This Is Knotting and Splicing

Hin/Kampa/Hille

Hearst
Marine
Books

New York

First published in the United States in 1983

ISBN 0-914814-35-4
Printed in Italy

1 2 3 4 5 6 7 8 9 10

CONTENTS

KEY TO PHOTOGRAPHS

Each photograph and each caption is numbered. The first digits of the caption indicate the page on which the photograph appears. The final digit, which also appears in the lower left corner of the photo, indicates which picture is being referred to. For example, on page 14, there are two pictures. They are labelled 141 and 142.

Introduction

There have been many books showing knots and splices in all the world's languages. There are huge comprehensive ones with every tangle and loop imaginable. There are slim volumes with essential hitches - even plastic cards showing the bare necessities for sailors, mountaineers or sporstmen. Between these extremes, others jostle on the book shelves.

But none is in color. *This Is Knotting and Splicing* is unique, because the team which devised, wrote and photographed it in Holland, has unlaid ropes, colored each strand and thus shown, where applicable, the relative complexities of knotting and splicing. Where different lines, but no strands, are involved then equal care has been taken to use or create cordage of different color.

The book has been written by **Floris Hin** with photography by **Theo Kampa** and **Jaap Hille**. The Dutch editor is **Wim de Bruijn**. Help in acquiring the many types of line was given by **Peter Kühne** of Marlow Ropes and **J. Wethman** of Lankhorst.

The book spans simple knots to time consuming plaited work and looks at the traditional hitches as well as the latest invention in the world of knots - designed to counteract the slipperiness of some synthetics - the Hunter's Bend. It is not often knots make front-page news in national dailies, but this one did on its invention in 1978, in the London *Times*.

The use of color to solve the age-old difficulty of explaining on paper the construction of knots, bends, hitches, whippings and splices has been made possible because Hearst Marine Books has produced this book as one of its THIS IS series. So a big printing in English, Dutch, German, Italian, Spanish and Swedish has been made, following existing all-color books on subjects such as racing, wind-surfing, sailboat cruising, diving, roughweather sailing and photography afloat. Meanwhile the first of the series, *This Is Sailing*, remains in print in twelve languages after thirteen years. Though rope materials change, most knots are likely to remains useful to successive generations. Hearst Marine Books is particularly pleased to have added this subject to its unique list.

SOME SUITABLE TOOLS FOR WORK ON ROPE

A Marline spike (with shackle spanner)

A conical metal spike is used to make a space between two parts of a rope, or to raise strands when splicing. The point can also be used to turn shackle pins with eyes, and to ease and free knots that have pulled tight. This stainless steel spike incorporates a shackle spanner. The material of which a marline spike or fid is made, depends on the material with which it will be used; a harder spike is needed for splicing steel wire rope than for rope.

B Marline spike

This conical metal tool may have a wooden or plastic handle; sometimes the handle and the tapering spike are forged in one piece. Photograph 511 shows a marline spike in use.

C Hollow splicing tool

This hollow spike is particularly handy for splicing steel wire rope, and is available in many types and sizes, with wooden or plastic handles. It is also ideal for splicing stiff rope, and for working on very tight knots. Great care is needed to avoid cutting any fibres or filaments of rope with the side edges, which are sometimes rather sharp. It is as well to round off the sides of a new tool with a file. Photographs 511 and 621 show a splicing tool in use.

D Fid

This pointed, conical tool is made of hard wood, and is used only when working with sailcloth or ropes, generally of larger diameter. The larger the rope, the bigger the fid should be; at two-thirds of its length, from the point, its diameter should be about the same as the diameter of the strand under which it will be pushed.

E Fid

This fid is bigger than fid D, and is required for heavier rope. Fids of all sizes are made of almost all materials (marline spikes being made of metal), such as hard wood, ash, nylon, plastic, ivory or horn.

Using splicing tools, marline spikes and fids

As opposed to the method of splicing and knotting generally described, I push the point of the tool away from me, and the strand towards me (photograph 621A), so that the thinnest part of the spike emerges between the strands at the point where I shall be pushing the strand in. The advantage of this is that, if the spike has been pushed through far enough for the strand to enter the opening, there will be plenty of space beneath the raised strand for the working strand to pass right through. The method is also handy when you are using a hollow splicing tool, as in photographs 511 and 621A. The strand being tucked in is placed in the groove of the tool (621A) and held down firmly with the thumb, so that

it can be pulled through beneath the raised strand. You therefore only need to make one movement to pull out the spike and simultaneously manipulate the working strand beneath the strand in the standing part.

When you are unable to make enough space using only the hollow spike (e.g. when you are making a very stiff knot), you can enlarge the gap with a solid steel marline spike until you have room to slip the working strand through (photograph 511B). When doing this, hold one tool in your left hand, and the other in your right.

Warning Always push the pointed end of a marline spike, fid or splicing tool away from you so that you will not hurt yourself if it slips out unexpectedly. Also never use a spike to turn a shackle unless it passes completely through the eye of the pin.

F Knife

Use a sharp knife with a good handle and a broad blade. To keep the blade sharp, carry in your tool bag either a whetstone or a piece of wood with fine-grade carborundum paper glued to it. A broad blade is better for cutting thick rope because the knife is less likely to slip. A blade with a straight back is very useful for folding back sailcloth in order to make a seam. Stainless steel is rather a soft metal and loses its edge easily. I prefer a good quality steel blade, and you can prevent rust by regular use, by polishing it with fine emery paper, or by oiling or greasing it.

One disadvantage of a clasp knife is the risk that it may close while you are using it — and it then traps your fingers usually! Another failing is that you cannot push the spike of a clasp knife through an object without damaging your hands.

G Cutters
Modern all-purpose shears. Use them only to cut thin sail thread or whipping twine, or possibly canvas. Do **NOT** use them for larger rope or wire; the former may force the jaws apart sideways and damage the shears, and the latter will dent and blunt the cutting edges.

H Pliers
Multi-purpose tool with an unlimited number of uses. They can be used for pulling strands or needles through rope or material when thumbs and fingers are unable to do so. Many sailors, sailmakers and riggers use pointed pincers with round cheeks.

I Wrench
I use this tool for the same purposes as pliers.

In order to pull the strands of very large rope really tight, you can use a bench vice instead of pliers. Clamp a strand in the vice, with the knot close by the jaws of the vice. Twist the strand (clockwise with right-hand lay rope: this term is explained at 141) and, inserting a screwdriver or marline spike between the vice and the knot, jerk the knot upwards to pull the strand really tight.

J Sailmaker's palm, Roping palm
Palms are made for both right-handed and left-handed people, and are put on like a glove. The round indented socket, which lies on the palm of the hand, can be used to push a needle easily through the material being sewn. There are many types, such as the sailmaker's palm, which generally has a very broad leather strap so as to protect the side of the hand and the little finger when thread is pulled taut.

K Sail needles
Made in various sizes. The size of the needle selected will depend on the size of the thread and on the cloth or rope to be sewn. Needles are graded numerically: the higher the number, the smaller the needle; the smaller the needle the thinner the yarn and the lighter the material or the smaller the rope to be worked on. Sail needles vary in (British) size from 6 to 18; we generally use numbers 15 or 16, and for heavier work below 12.

Needles can be kept in a home-made copper or brass case, the base being a wooden bung that fits inside the tube, to which it is riveted with a nail. The bung must be wooden so as to avoid damaging the tips of the needles. A wooden stopper closes the other end of the tube.

L Tarred twine
Thin, strong, smooth twine is twisted from yarns made of flaxen fibres. Sail thread and whipping twine are made in various sizes, according to what they will be used for; there may be two or three different yarns in one length of twine, which may or may not be tarred. There is also —

M Twine and thread made of synthetic fibres
It is usual to use fibre twine for cloth and/or rope made of natural fibres, and synthetic twine for synthetic cloth and/or rope.

N Adhesive Tape
Good masking tape can be used to save the trouble of whipping the ends of the rope or of strands, and to stop them from unlaying and untwisting while knots or splices are being made. Smoother tape is preferable because it is easier to work with.

O Transparent adhesive tape e.g. Sellotape
Effectively prevents the ends from unravelling, especially when working with thin rope.

P Sheath
To take knife F, pliers H, marline spike A and splicing tool C. Yachting kits can be obtained in chandler's stores and may consist of pliers, screwdrivers, knife or spike.

The following tools, which are not illustrated, can also be useful:
- a little board on which to cut rope, so that you do not blunt the edge of your knife.
- a gas cigarette lighter for melting together the filaments at the ends of synthetic fibre ropes. You can do this with an old kitchen knife, heated in a flame; sailmakers and riggers often use an electrically heated knife, or a special tool that melts the filaments.

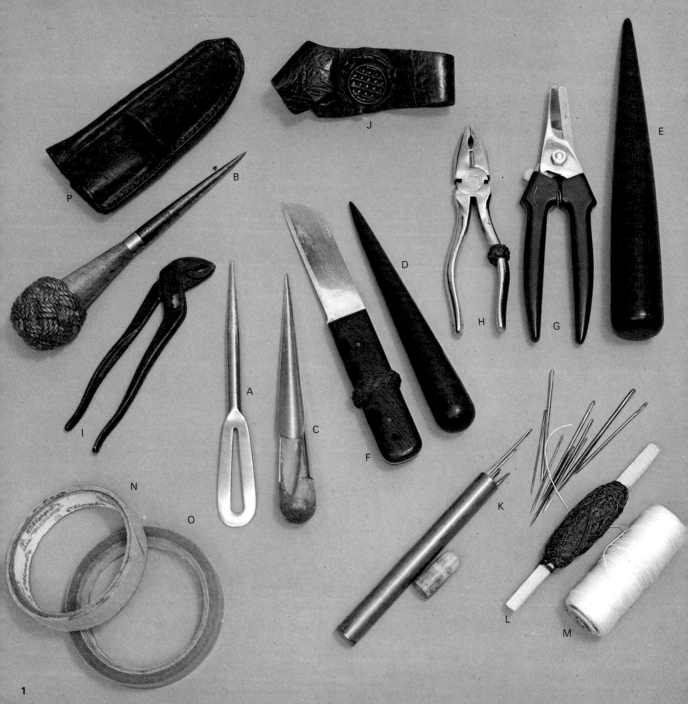

1

9

ROPES

One old type of rope is hemp rope. It is the strongest of the ropes that are made of natural fibres, and like all natural rope weathers badly. This can be partly countered by tarring the rope with Stockholm tar. Although this initially slightly reduces its strength, the greater durability of tarred hemp means that it is not long before it actually becomes stronger than untarred hemp.

Although plain and tarred hemp rope are virtually obsolete, it can fortunately still be obtained here and there in specialist shops.

Wet hemp, and other ropes made of natural fibres, must always be dried hanging up, clear of the ground and away from a wall. Stow the rope where the wind can circulate right through it, preferably hanging in a dark place away from direct sunlight.

The tensile strength of hemp, relative to tarred hemp and manila, is approximately 100:75:80.

Manila 102
Manila rope too is a natural fibre rope, and is still seen around. Fortunately the owners of some traditional sailing boats still prefer to use manila in their rigging, and it is often used for decorative work still. Manila is used relatively more frequently than hemp in spite of being 20 per cent less strong, partly because it can be obtained in larger sizes more easily, and also because it weathers better than hemp.

Polypropylene 103
Polypropylene rope can be used as a cheap substitute for other synthetic and natural fibres. It has poor resistance to abrasion, and therefore must be prevented from chafing. Polypropylene rope can be knotted and spliced rather easily as it is soft

Polyethylene (111)

Polyethylene has many of the same characteristics as polypropylene, but it is extremely difficult to knot because it stretches so much, loses shape so easily and is very slippery. After a knot has been undone, the kinks stay in the rope for a long time, and the consequence is that the rope, being hard to coil, becomes unmanageable. The kinks can be removed from the rope if it is stretched out on a sunny day and left for an hour or so. It has commercial use, but is not recommended for sailing, mountaineering or other demanding sports.

on the hands. It has an advantage in that it is buoyant. It is advisable to get rid of polypropylene rope, especially ropes that are light in colour, for they are very sensitive to ultra-violet rays. Be careful not to mistake it for Terylene, which is far superior.

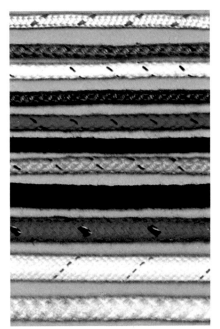

Polyester 112

Polyester ropes, which are very well known under the names of Terylene and Dacron, are the third strongest of the man-made fibre ropes, after Kevlar and nylon. The low stretch factor — which can be further reduced by special treatment during manufacture, means that the rope is extremely suitable for activities where minimal stretch is required. Plaited or braided, polyester rope is easy to handle and used for almost all purposes in the running rigging of a boat. Three-strand Terylene is strong, chafe resistant and very long wearing for warps and other heavy duty.

Polyamide 113

Polyamide is widely known as nylon, which is actually a technical name. Nylon is slightly stronger than Terylene of the same diameter and on account of its great elasticity, it is used when it is necessary to absorb heavy shocks. The rope becomes hard in excessive sunlight. Greater care is needed when knotting and splicing polyamide because of its elasticity and slipperiness and an extra tuck or additional half-hitch should be made for safety.

Kevlar (not illustrated)

This Du Pont aromatic polyamide fibre has the highest strength against its weight or diameter of any fibre used in ropes. It has virtually no stretch. It resists ultra-violet light when in a polyester jacket. There is only a five per cent loss of strength when spliced. Pale gold in colour, it is used for halyards, spinnaker guys and control lines, though not for sheets. It is much more expensive than other synthetic rope.

		Specific gravity	Floats	Water absorption when the rope is immersed	Moisture regain	Rotproofness	Chemical properties; whether affected or not	Affected by sunlight, ultra-violet rays	Softening point	Melting point	Abrasion resistance	Elongation at break as a %
1	**COTTON**	Over 1	No	High	Yes	Very bad	Yes	Yes	Chars and burns		Bad	
2	**SISAL**	1.25	No	High	Yes	Very bad	Yes	Yes	Chars and burns		Moderate	±13
3	**MANILA**	1.5-1.6	No	High	Yes	Very bad to bad	Yes	Yes	Chars and burns		Moderate to good	±13
4	**HEMP**	Over 1.5	No	High	Yes	Untarred- very bad; tarred- moderate	Yes	Yes	Chars and burns		Bad	
5	**POLYETHYLENE**	0.95	Yes	±25% of own weight	No	Good	No	Yes	100-120°	130°	Small sizes bad, thicker moderate	20-30
6	**POLYPROPYLENE** three-stranded laid	0.91	Yes	±20% of own weight	No	Good	No	Yes, especially lighter colours	135°	165°	Small sizes bad, thicker moderate	10-25
7	**POLYPROPYLENE** braided	0.91	Yes	±20% of own weight	No	Good	No	Yes, especially lighter colours	135°	165°	Small sizes bad, thicker moderate	10-25
8	**POLYESTER** three-stranded laid	1.38	No	±50% of own weight	No	Good	No	Minimal	230°	230-260°	Moderate	5-25
9	**POLYESTER** double-braided	1.38	No	±50% of own weight	No	Good	No	Minimal	230°	230-260°	Moderate	5-25
10	**POLYAMIDE** braided	1.14	No	±60% of own weight	No	Good	Yes, dissolves in hydrochloric acid	Yes, especially in thinner sizes	180-235°	195-260°	Moderate	to ca
11	**POLYAMIDE**	1.14	No	±60% of own weight	No	Good	Yes, dissolves in hydrochloric acid	Yes, especially in thinner sizes	180-235°	195-265°	Moderate	to ca
12	**KEVLAR** kevlar core, braided polyester sheath	0.55	Depends on construction		No	Good	No		Chars at 350°		Very bad	Max 2-3

Wet strength as a % of dry	Residual breaking strength when knotted	Breaking strength in pounds, diameter given in inches X = not generally available in this size											
		3/32		3/16		1/4	5/16	3/8	1/2	9/16	5/8	3/4	13/16
		45	55	120	145	220	420	510	880	230	x	x	x
105		Best quality sisal is generally as strong as manila											
105		x	x	275	440	600	105	1400	2050	2800	4000	4850	6270
86		x	x	340	440	615	1100	1570	2200	2980	4180	4840	6550
	±60%	x	x	420	625	900	1630	2300	3170	4350	5770	7260	8990
± 99	±55%	x	x	495	880	1170	2000	3000	4250	5775	7380	9460	11365
± 99	±55%	Depending on how it is braided is generally less strong than three-strand laid.											
±100	±50%	x	x	625	860	1250	2170	3330	4820	6600	8560	10900	13640
±100	±50%	Depending on how it is braided and the way the rope is assembled, is generally the same strength as or stronger than three-stranded laid rope											
±100	±60%	330	440	660	1100	1715	2860	4290	5940	7900	10550	x	x
±100	±60%	x	x	750	1155	1650	2970	4575	6600	9000	11660	14740	18250
100	NEVER KNOT	x	x	1365	1925	2200	3410	9900	15540	19560	21960	23100	x

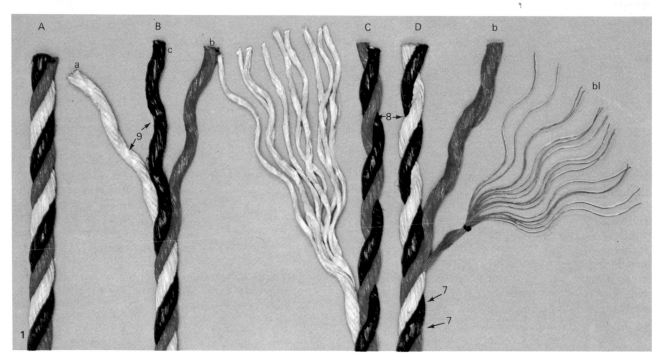

ROPE CONSTRUCTION 141

A. Three strands laid right-handed to make cable-laid rope. In other words, the strands slope away to the right when you look at the photograph and you follow them upwards.

B. The three individual strands, a, b and c.

C. Yarns twisted left-handed to make a strand, here the yellow strand Ca, left.

D. Fibres spun right-handed to make a yarn.

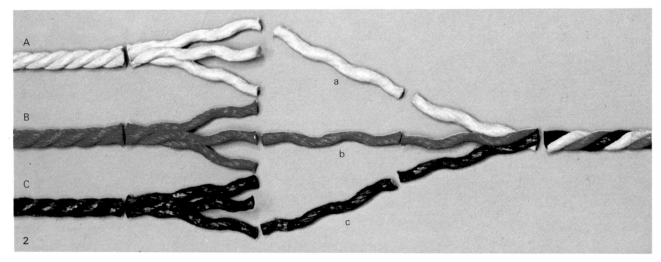

THREE-COLORED ROPE 142

Three-colored rope (see introduction) is frequently used in this book and I had to construct it because it is not available commercially.

To do the same, take three lengths of rope (142 A, B, C) of different colors and unlay one strand from each (142 a, b, c). Holding the ends together in your left hand, re-lay these three strands in turn with your right hand, twisting each strand firmly and away from you as you lay it towards you with the crimped strands (141 B9) facing towards the centre and the matching crimped strands with the other strands. To avoid tangles, do not use overlong pieces of rope. Use three pieces of single-colored rope 3 ft. long.

TERMS USED 151

- *Standing part* (151A1 and 151B1) comes from a fixed point, whether attached or not.
- A bend of over 180 degrees in a rope is termed a *bight*. (151A2)
- A closed loop is also a *bight* or an *eye* (151A3 and 151B3)
- The tail being used is often called the *bitter end* or *bare end* (151A4 and 151B4)
- It is called this all the time and as it passes over or under the standing part (151A5)
- The cantline or contline is the spiral groove between two strands occurring when one strand is unlaid from rope. See 141C8 – in which the yellow strand, and 141D8, the orange strand, lay. The 'crimped' part (141B9) is where a strand was in contact with the other two strands.

HOW TO FOLLOW THE PHOTOGRAPHS 151

Two methods have been used to make it easy to see how ropes or strands cross one another:

- A differently colored whipping is applied to the bare end so that you can follow the movements from start to finish (151A).
- It is not the bitter end of the rope that is used to belay a rope to a cleat (461–471) or a belaying pin (481), as it might appear from the photographs. For greater clarity I have eliminated all the tail of the rope that has not yet been passed round the cleat or belaying pin, and I have applied a plastic sleeve of a different color to the end; in fact, there would still be several yards of rope beyond the yellow band.
- Ropes are colored differently where they cross each other.

The end of a rope is whipped so as to prevent it from looking like a dishmop when it unravels. To avoid wastage, especially when you have a number of ropes or lines, such as reef points or lacing lines, to be whipped one after the other, apply the whipping twine direct from the container or spool, and cut it off close by the rope when you have finished.

You can take the turns round the rope towards you or away from you when you apply the whipping; in practice it makes no difference which. If the loop starts to kink when you are heaving it taut (F, G, H, I), you can guide the twine by inserting the point of your spike in the bight. If a smooth whipping is required, first smooth the twine itself by smearing it with a little beeswax or a spot of tallow. The length of the whipping should be about $1\frac{1}{2}$ times the diameter of the rope.

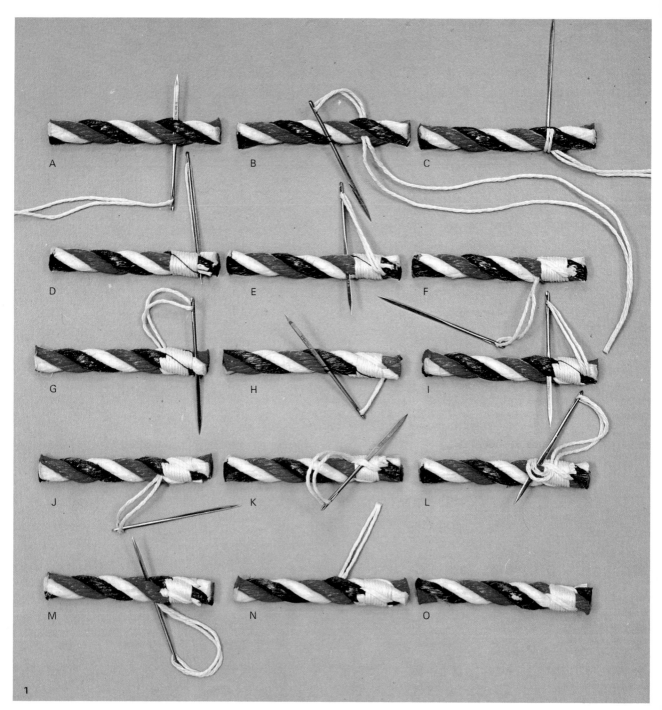

A　　　　　　B　　　　　　C

D　　　　　　E　　　　　　F

G　　　　　　H　　　　　　I

J　　　　　　K　　　　　　L

M　　　　　　N　　　　　　O

1

SEWN WHIPPING AND SAILMAKER'S WHIPPING 181

With sewn whipping the turns are held when you pass the twine over them along the contline, indicated by the black thread in D, E, G, H and I), and you sew it across the strands with the needle. With sailmaker's whipping no needle is used, the rope being unlaid and a bight left at the start of the whipping before the turns are taken. This bight encircles a strand and, when the turns are complete, is passed over the same strand and then hauled tight; the ends are knotted beyond the whipping with a reef knot.

Both whippings must be longer than the diameter of the rope; sewn is finished by knotting the twine (L), and sewing the remainder through the rope several times (M).

The sewn whippings cannot slip off the end of smooth rope. When applied to braided and double-braided ropes instead of spiralling up between the strands, it should be spaced out crosswise round the circumference. Core and sheath must be stitched together.

FLAT SEIZING 191

Sew the rope together to form an eye of the right size, making three or four stitches (A, B, C). Take round turns round both ropes until the seizing is about 1½–2 times as long as the diameter of the doubled rope; follow this by making three cross-turns (D, E, F, G) and haul the whole seizing tight. Finish by using up the remaining twine (H, I, J).

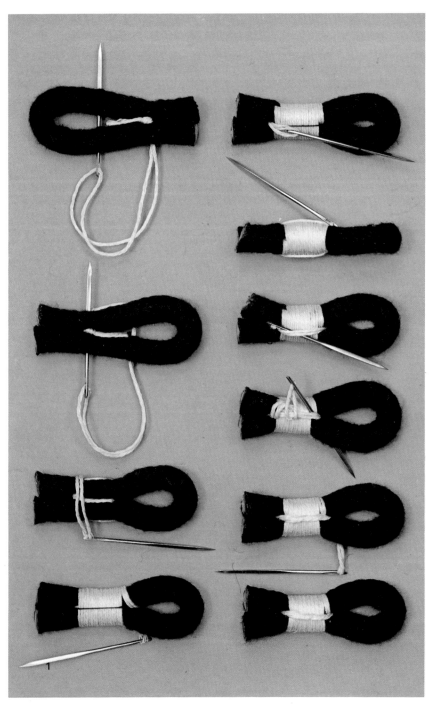

A

B

1

C

OVERHAND KNOT or
THUMB KNOT 201, 202

The overhand or thumb knot is a stopper knot, and is made to prevent a rope such as the uphaul of a sailboard (202) from slipping through your hands. It may also be made if a rope is not to slip through a ring, eye or hole.

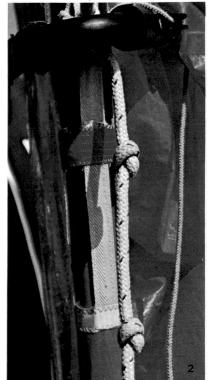

2

FIGURE OF EIGHT
KNOT 211, 212

The figure of eight knot is thicker and therefore more efficient than the overhand knot. It is also preferable because it does not jam as tight and is always very easily undone, even after being subjected to a great load.

Two half hitches (221A, B, C, D)
Two half hitches, the first a slip hitch (222A, B)
Two half hitches made with doubled line (223A, B)

A

B

C

D

1

1 A B   2 A B C

Fisherman's bend (231A, B)
Round turn and two half hitches (232A, B, C)

Basically these are all the same. The first half hitch is slipped (222A) when you need to be able to free the hitch easily. When the rope is long, the hitch is made with doubled rope (223A) to save having to pull it all through. The fisherman's bend (231) is most often used when making semi-permanent mooring lines fast, or when bending the anchor cable to the anchor ring.

TWO INCORRECT HALF HITCHES 233

The second hitch has been led the wrong way.

3

CLOVE HITCH 241A, B
251C, D, 242, 243

The clove hitch is used to attach a rope (say a mooring rope) to an object such as a mooring post or ring.

It is usual to take a round turn clockwise with right-hand lay rope; this is the opposite way to that shown in photographs 241 and 251 where the turns were taken anti-clockwise because the hitch would

have been hidden by the post. The round turns are made correctly, clockwise, in photographs 242 and 243.

After passing the line around the post or the rope, be sure to take end (a) beneath standing part (b) (241A) before taking the second turn around the post or rope (241B, 251C), because otherwise the hitch

will be awkward to complete and, more important, much more difficult to free.

A half hitch can be added around the standing part (251D) to prevent the clove hitch from working loose as a result of the vessel's motion and the smoothness of the rope.

24

ROLLING HITCH 252

A rolling hitch is made when a line under load must not slip along a spar or another rope, for example to secure a pendant to a shroud, a stay or the mast, a halyard to the yard or gaff of a sailing dinghy such as an Optimist, or to secure the line beneath the flag that holds it to the flagstaff, or individual towropes to a central towrope when a number of boats are towed in pairs.

In the photograph the load is applied to the standing part from the right. Take a round turn (252A), and follow this with a turn between the round turn and the standing part (252B, C) before finishing in the same way as you normally finish a clove hitch (252D, E, F). If the central rope (a), or the object, is very smooth, add an extra round turn or two between stages 252B and 252D before finishing with a clove hitch (252G). Alternatively you can make the hitch more secure by making half hitches on the standing part.

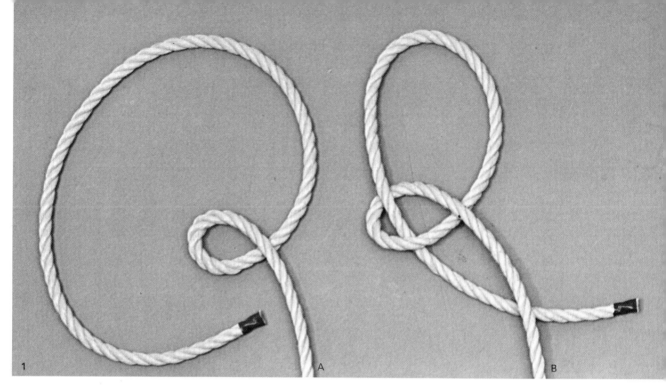

1   A   B

BOWLINE   261, 271

A bowline is made when a non-slip loop is required, for example in a mooring rope, a warp, or a towrope. You will have no difficulty over making the knot if you study photographs 261 and 271.

To lengthen a tow-rope or anchor cable, you make a bowline in the ends of both ropes, with the loops interlocking like chain links. This important knot is used among many other things to attach the sheet to the clew of a headsail. (272)

If the rope is very slippery, or for additional security, make one or two half hitches round the bight (b) with the end (a), as is always done by mountaineers.

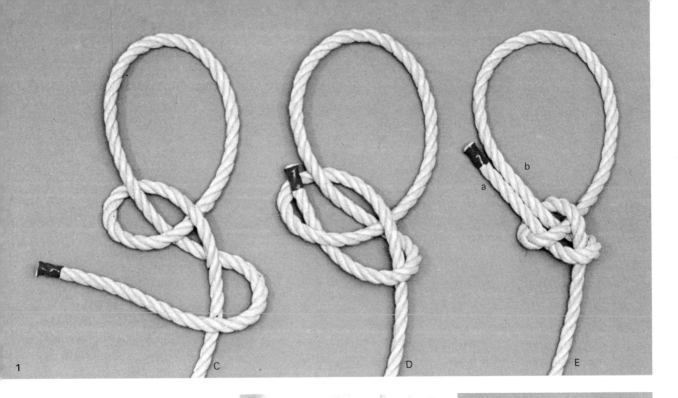

1   C   D   E

FIGURE OF EIGHT KNOT TIED IN DOUBLED END 273

This is a useful knot to tie in smooth rope and thin line. It holds very well and is extremely easily undone, even after being under a very heavy load.

3   A   B

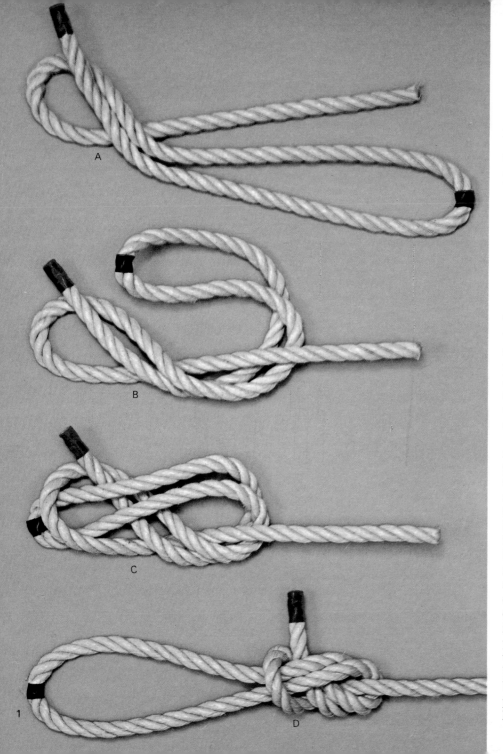

FIGURE OF EIGHT KNOT TIED IN DOUBLED END Second variation, 281

A similar knot to 273. It can be made quickly in thin slippery line to provide a loop, and is used by anglers to make a non-slip loop.

BOWLINE ON THE BIGHT 291

When making a bowline on the bight, a problem may arise at stage 291C; you must pass the large black loop right behind the knot and then heave the knot tight by pulling the small double loop (a) towards you.

This knot is made in the middle of a long warp to provide a non-slip loop that can be placed over a mooring post amidships; the two ends are then brought back on board to serve as fore and aft springs. The bowline on the bight may be made in the doubled end of a halyard as a boatswains's chair. You sit in the larger outer loop, while the shorter inside loop passes round your back. Enough of the working end (291E a) must be pulled through for it to be secured to the standing part (b) with two half hitches.

A

B

C

D

1

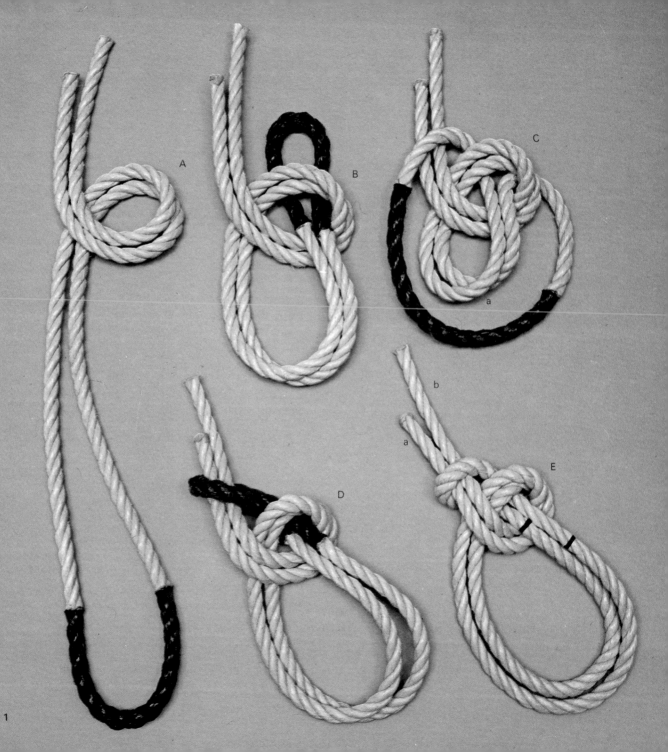

1

REEF or SQUARE KNOT 301

The reef or square knot is used to connect two ropes of the same size. It has a disadvantage in that it can be pulled extremely tight and be difficult to undo, but the back of the knot can be broken by taking adjacent parts – either red end (a) and standing part (b) or yellow (c) and (d) – and pulling them in opposite directions.

This makes a reef knot: left over right (301A) – twist through (301B) – right over left (301C) – twist through (301D) – haul tight.

If the rope is extremely smooth the knot can be made more secure by tying one or two half hitches with ends (a) and (c) around standing parts (b) and (d). The term reef knot stems from the fact that it was

A

B
1

formerly used to tie the reef points round the bunt of the sail. It is a knot that can slip and for safety two bowlines are recommended when joining lines.

SLIP REEF KNOT 302

If you leave a loop in the end of 301C – as in 311A, you make a slip knot as illustrated in 302. This is very easy to free, and may be used whenever something has to be secured quickly and efficiently but temporarily.

A slip reef knot may be made in the Terylene sail tyers when furling a sail.

REEF BOW 311

This well-known knot, used to tie two ends together, is made daily in tying shoe laces. When rope or line is extremely smooth, pull the loops through to make a normal reef knot, which holds better.

SINGLE 321 I and DOUBLE 321 II SHEET BEND

This is first and foremost the bend to use when connecting two ropes of different sizes. Always make the bight with the thicker rope, and bend the thinner rope to it. If the rope is very smooth, do not rely on the single sheet bend, but use a double – or even treble sheet bend. Is now used most frequently to attach a flag to a flagline.

FISHERMAN'S KNOT or DOUBLE THUMB KNOT, or ENGLISHMAN'S KNOT 331 and DOUBLE FISHERMAN'S KNOT 332

The fisherman's knot is a good alternative to the reef knot, and is useful when knotting two lines together, especially when they are of small diameter. It is used by fishermen when mending nets.

If the material is particularly slippery, such as nylon fishing line, the double fisherman's knot can be used.

CARRICK BEND 341

This is used when bending two heavier warps to each other and, to fulfil this purpose, the ends (a and c) MUST be stopped (e) to the standing parts (b and d). See flat seizing, photograph 191. Thickness is only increased slightly with a carrick bend, and the knot will run through a hawse hole or over a warping drum without this bend. It is easily freed once the stopping has been released.

DOUBLE CARRICK
BEND 342–352, 351

The double carrick bend will only hold when the ends (a and c) are stopped (e) to the standing parts (b and d).

The diamond knot made with two ropes (381/391) is based on the double carrick bend.

In macramé, which is a type of decorative knot-work, this much-used knot is called the Josephine.

HUNTER'S BEND 361,
371

This new bend, introduced in 1978 by Dr Edward Hunter, is used to join lines made of smooth, synthetic materials, and can be used as an alternative to a sheet bend.

The start (361A–E) is simple enough, but the following movements (as shown in 371F–M) are rather more tricky. You can see in the series of photographs how the knot turns about itself as you haul carefully on the standing parts and turn the end towards you. When tight the front will look like L, and the back like M.

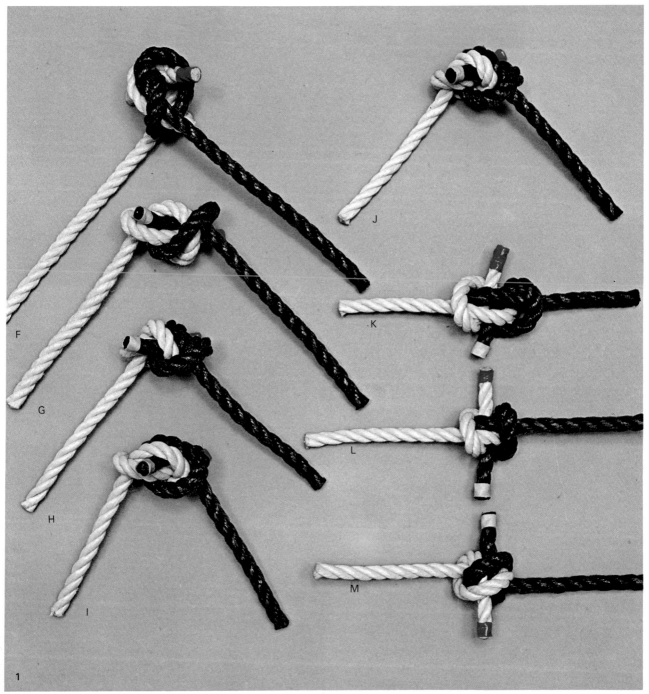

F

G

H

I

J

K

L

M

1

37

A

B

C

1

DIAMOND KNOT, MADE WITH TWO ROPES 381–391

This decorative knot is made to form a bight in a rope, and is often used for a lanyard for a marline spike or for some other tool, or to attach a whistle to a lifejacket.

You can also vary it by unlaying the two lines (b and c) beneath the knot, and plaiting the strands

together by some method (as used for sennits).

The knot (381A) starts with a double carrick bend. The ends are then passed round and up through the centre of the bend from below. This central point is easy to recognize because it is rectangular in

shape. Gradually pull the slack out of the bights, and haul the knot tight slowly (391D, E). This must be done with great care to avoid a Gordion knot at the half way stage! 391F shows the finished diamond knot.

HEAVING LINE KNOT 401

When a line has to be thrown to the shore or to another vessel, the end of it can be weighted by making a heaving line knot.

Another use for this knot is to make a knob at one end of a short piece of rope; this is thrust through an eye at the other end, and the strop can be used, say, to hang sails or rope on the guardrail. (741)

Personally, I make heaving line knots at the end of the main and mizzen sheets, and at the inboard ends of the heaving line, the log line of a chip log, and the lead line. It is also a convenient knot to make at the ends of drawstrings in clothing, kit bags, lacings etc to prevent them from being pulled right out.

COILING THE HEAVING LINE 411

One-quarter inch thick, supple, untarred three-stranded hemp makes a fine heaving line. Braided synthetic line without a core, made of buoyant polyethylene or polypropylene fibres, is also extremely satisfactory.

A heaving line must fly out well when released, and it therefore has to be coiled carefully with the minimum of kinks and crossed turns, and with each bight smaller than the one before so that it will not catch at all. Be sure not to let go of the standing end, and preferably make it fast to something on board.

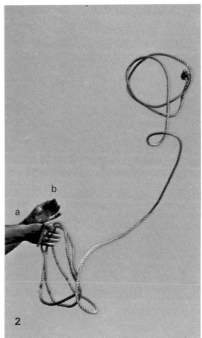

THROWING THE HEAVING LINE 412

Divide the coil of rope between your hands, holding the half with the heaving line knot in your throwing hand (411b, 412b); the other half is in your other hand, which keeps a firm hold of the standing end (411a, 412a).

You can throw the line underhand or overhand. Provided there is enough room, an underhand throw is preferable because you can aim better. However you may have to throw overarm if you are standing close to a bulwark or rail, and both methods should be practised so that you can make contact with the shore effectively from the boat. Like the thrower in the photograph, you may be left-handed, and if so you have to coil the line even more carefully.

MONKEY'S FIST 431

A good method of weighting the throwing end of the heaving line is to make a monkey's fist, which for the purposes of illustration in photograph 431, is in ⅜ in. line. To make the photograph clearer, the knot is shown as being made up of 3 × 2 round turns, but in practice you will actually make it with 3 × 3 round turns, as in photograph 421. You can make the monkey's fist at the end of the heaving line itself, but this makes it difficult to bend the heaving line to a warp, and it is awkward when led through a hawse hole or fairhead. An alternative is shown in photograph 421.

After making the monkey's fist, carefully pulling the knot tight, bight by bight and turn by turn, splice the two ends together (421a) with a short splice (as in 531). The loop formed can be seized (as in 191) centrally, or you could splice

the two lines together first as in 421; the total length is 12–16 in.

The knot can also be worked round a small hard rubber ball, to enable it to be thrown in high winds as well.

Just as with the heaving line knot, a monkey's fist can be used for a knob and eye strop (741). An eye splice is then made at one end and, at the other, a monkey's fist that just squeezes through the eye.

A short strop like this can be seized (191) or knotted centrally with a clove hitch to a lifeline, for example; it can then be used to hold sheets, sails and mooring ropes free of the deck but ready for use.

The monkey's fist can also be used effectively to thicken the end of any control line. When made round a cork core, it makes a first class key pendant which will float (862).

A

B

C

D

E

F

1

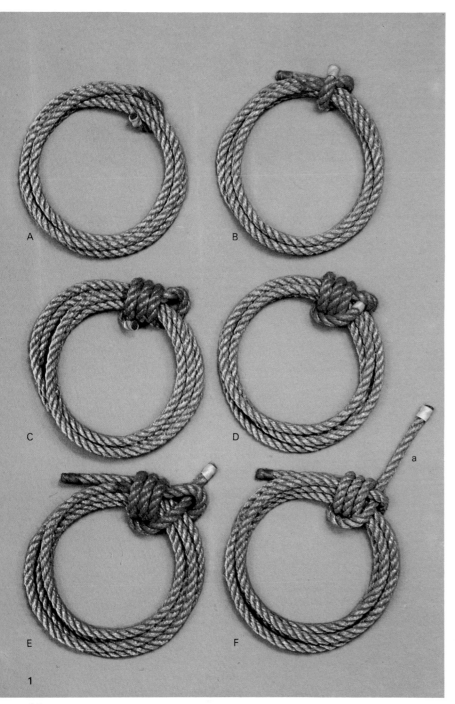

COILING A ROPE 441

If you leave a coiled synthetic fibre rope out in the sun regularly, it becomes deformed by the heat of the sun and later, when you want to use it, there seems to be nothing but kinks and cross turns in the rope. Photograph 441 shows one way of avoiding kinks.

If you intend to secure a coiled sheet to a lifeline, guardrail, eye or ring, be sure that the end marked (a) is long enough.

COILING A ROPE WITH A BIGHT 451

A bight on the end of a rope can be used to keep the rope coiled tidily or to hang it up, and the bight comes immediately to hand when you take the rope to put it to use.

A bight in a mooring rope should be at least 20–30 in. long in order to pass over bollards and posts in locks and harbours.

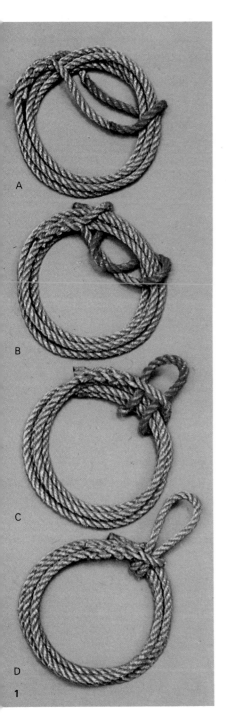

A

B

C

D

1

A   B   C   D

1

BELAYING A ROPE TO A CLEAT 461–471

Every single rope on board will doubtless have to be made fast somewhere at some time.

The protruding parts of a cleat (a, b) are the horns. The cleat must be big enough for the rope to pass beneath the horns at least three or four times, after which a half hitch is added for security.

When belaying, it is the three or four cross turns (461B, C, D), taken before the half hitch (471E, F, G) is made, that are important. The half hitch is added purely to ensure that the turns do not fall off as a result of the boat's motion, and there must be NO load whatsoever on the half hitch because it would then become

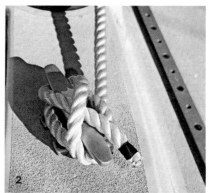

2

46

1   E   F   G

jammed tight; the rope could then only be released with great difficulty in case of need.

When a cleat is fitted vertically, take the half hitch on the upper horn, and when it is fitted horizontally, on the horn pointing towards the standing part of the line or rope being belaid.

In the photographs, the tail of the rope has been omitted in order to show more clearly the movements made with the rope; at each stage the rope beyond the yellow sleeve has been cut off.

The cleat is sited at a slight angle to the direction of pull of the line being belaid, so as to make it easier

to make the rope fast, and to prevent the wood to which it is bolted from splitting.

1   A   B   C   D   E

BELAYING A ROPE TO A BELAYING PIN   481

A rope is made fast to a belaying pin in much the same way as to a cleat. With right-hand lay rope – and 99% of three-stranded rope on board is right-hand lay – start to the right of the pin or cleat and take a full round turn clockwise round the pin (481A) or cleat (461A, B). Turns are taken in the same direction as that in which rope is coiled (see photographs 441 and 451) because the strands are not then forced open so much, the rope kinks less, which means less chafe, and its strength is not reduced as a consequence of twisted yarns and strands.

Left-handed people must remember that they tend to belay anti-clockwise, although the rope is right-hand lay; if they then coil the rope anticlockwise too, this will cause twists and kinks to form and

2

1

later, when the rope runs out, it will snarl up badly.

Braided rope can be coiled clockwise or anticlockwise without kinking, and can also be belaid either way. As on the cleat, it is the cross turns on the belaying pin (481B, C) that bear the load on the rope, not the half hitch (481D, E). The half hitch is added only to keep the turns (481E) in place, and it is always made above the fiferail, pinrail or mast band, namely, on the side nearer the standing part. To keep chafe to the minimum, round off the edges of the rail well; the diameter of the pin should be at least as great, but preferably greater, than the diameter of the rope being belaid.

BELAYING TO A BOLLARD 493

Here you lead the rope beneath the cross pin and take a couple of round turns round the bollard before finishing with several cross turns and a half hitch on the pin.

2

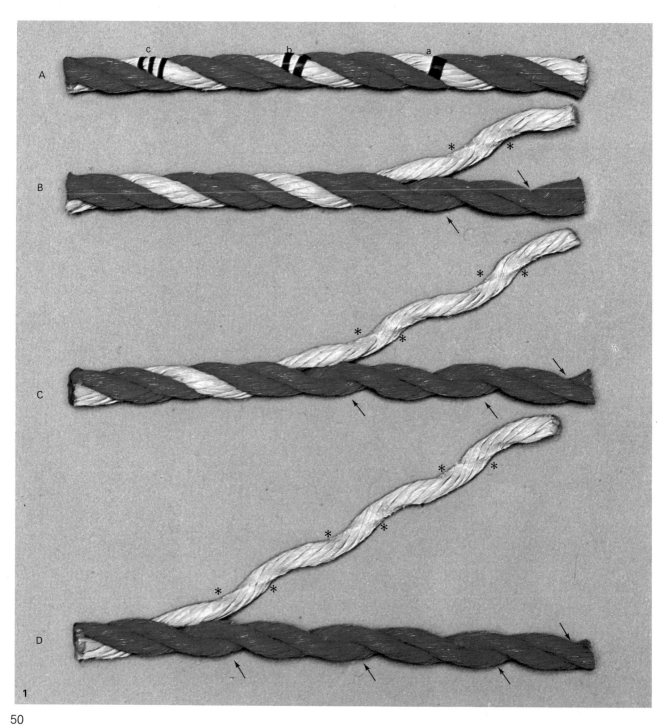

PREPARING TO SPLICE 501

In order to splice or to make a decorative knot, the rope is unlaid a certain distance. One 'turn' of 360° unlays the strand as far as the single band (a), two turns unlay it as far as the two bands (b) and three turns to (c) where three bands have been applied. In rope-making the distance from (a) to (b) and (b) to (c) is termed jaw, but splicing instructions more often relate the length of rope to be unlaid to the diameter or circumference of the rope itself – say about eight circumferences when making an eye splice with three to four tucks. When laying or re-laying rope, say a single strand when making a long splice (541–551) or grommet (581), hold the laid rope in your left hand, with the loose strand pointing to the right. With your right hand, twist the strand away from you stiffly as you lay it carefully in the groove between the two laid strands, checking that the part of the strand where the yarns and fibres are crimped beds down naturally in the groove, without being squeezed or distorted.

MAKING EXTRA SPACE TO TUCK A STRAND 511

You can increase the space through which the strand will be tucked by pushing the solid marline spike (x) and the hollow splicing tool (y) towards each other.

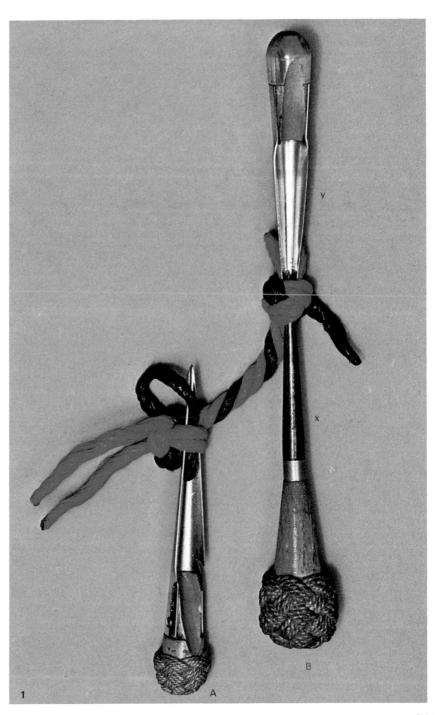

SHORT SPLICE 531

Mooring ropes frequently wear badly where they chafe against harbour walls, and unless you prevent this immediately the rope will have to be repaired. The easy way out is to cut out the chafed part, but what is left will then be too short for a mooring rope. The short splice is a better answer.

A short splice may also be used when making a strop (a rope loop), in which case you have to make three full turns in the rope, as if you were coiling it, before starting to splice; if you do not do this, you will have a cross turn in the finished strop after the splice has been completed.

The black thread in photographs 531A and B shows clearly how far the ropes have been unlaid, and how they are 'married' when they are thrust towards each other. When starting by working towards the left, secure the strands of the left hand rope around the right hand rope with tape (531C). Then tuck the three unlaid strands of the right hand rope (s, t, u), passing each strand over the adjacent strand in the left hand rope before tucking it under the strand next to that (531). Tuck the left hand rope strands (x, y, z) into the right hand rope (531E), and haul the tucks tight by pulling the working ends of

the strands in opposite directions; the left rope strands to the right, and the right rope strands to the left. Now tuck the strands to left and right again (531F). When splicing natural fibre rope, three tucks are needed after marrying the strands (531A, B, C), but five or six are needed if the material is very slippery.

The strands of both ropes may be tapered by cutting off one strand at every tuck (see photograph 711a).

1

2

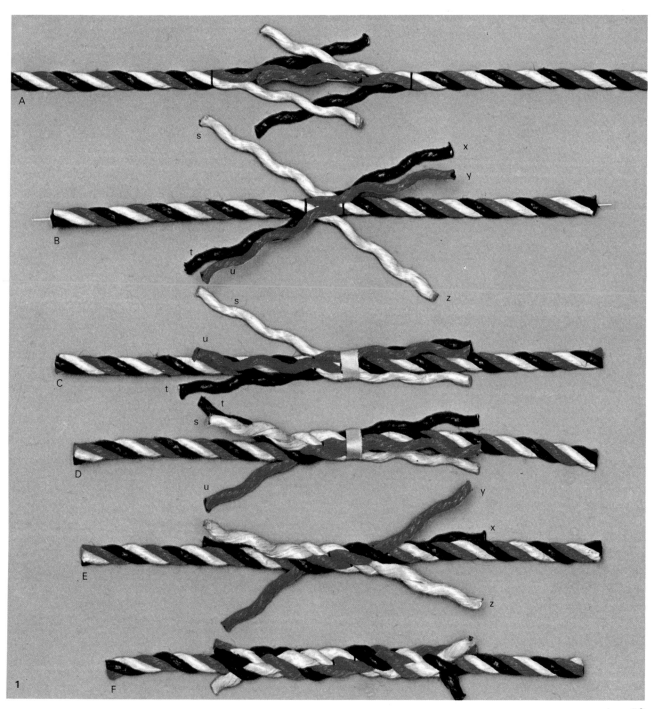

A

s

B
t
u
x
y
z

s

C
u
t

t
s
D
u

y
E
x
z

F

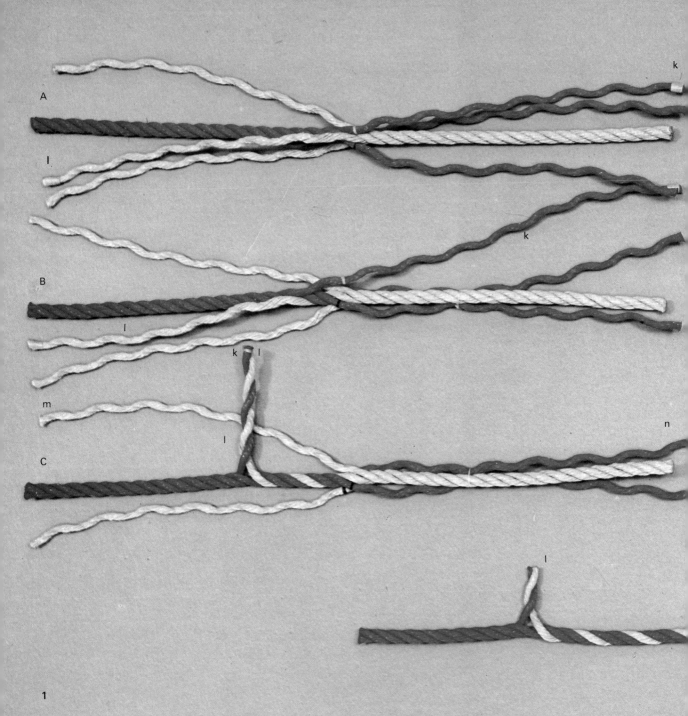

1

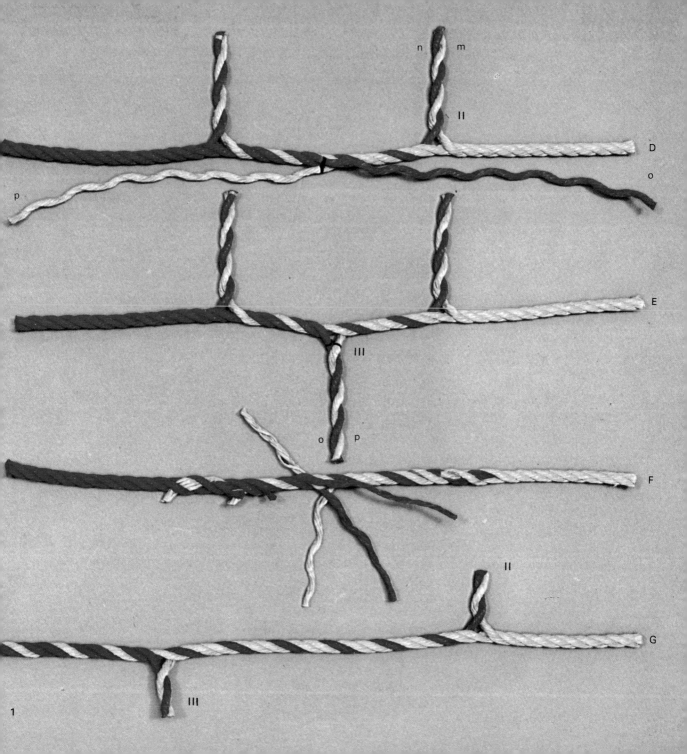

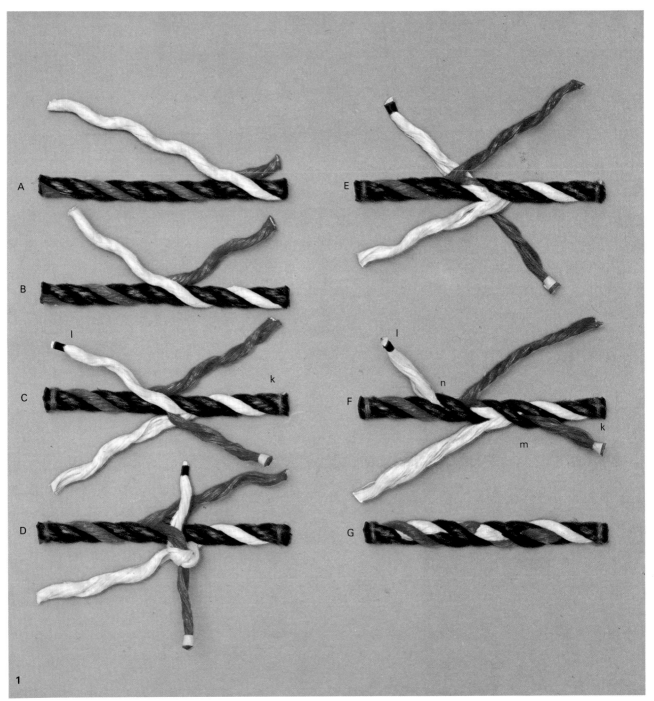

LONG SPLICE 541–551

A long splice is made to join two lines virtually invisibly, and with very little increase in diameter, as is required when running rigging is put through an eye or a block. The two ropes are unlaid for a distance of about 20–25 times the circumference, and married (541A). One strand (k) is then unlaid from the left rope, and the equivalent right hand rope strand (l) is laid in the groove that is left. Replace the left rope strand with the right rope strand until about 4 in. of the right strand remains. Twist the strands together, and cut them off to the same length (I in 541C). Now take a second pair of strands, one (m) from the right rope, the other (n) the left rope strand that lies opposite; repeat the process, this time towards the right (II in 551D). Twist the remaining two strands (o, p) together and cut them short at about 4 in. (III in 551E). In reality the three twisted pairs, I, II and III (551E, G) would be about a yard apart, the distance between I and II being about 6½ ft. These pairs are finished (551F) as shown in photograph 561.

FINISHING A LONG SPLICE AND A GROMMET 561

Halve both strands (561C). Place half of left strand (k) in front of half of right strand (l) and tie them together with an overhand knot (561D). When you haul the knot tight, it will drop right down between the strands (561E). Now place half-strand (k) over the space

that is left in the yellow strand beyond the knot, and tuck it beneath the adjacent black strand (m) – see 561F. Then take the half right strand (l) over the space beyond the knot in the orange strand, and tuck it beneath the adjacent black strand (n, see 561F). Pull the half strands tight so that no space is left beneath or near the strands. The half strands may be tucked once or several times, depending on the smoothness of the material. You can also pass each half over the strand next

to it, and then tuck it back immediately under the same strand.

Stretch the splice well by pulling the two ropes apart, roll or hammer it into shape, and then cut off the ends. With a natural fibre rope, cut the ends so as to leave about half a centimetre sticking out, but when using synthetic rope, melt the strands to form a small collar which will drop into the groove.

Photograph 571 shows a heaving line with a buoyant grommet attached to it, hung up ready for use.

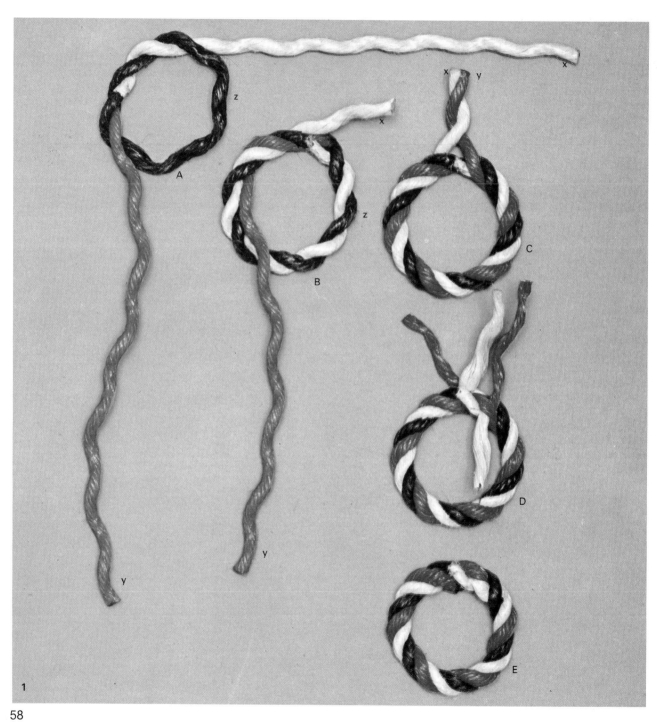

GROMMET 581

A grommet is a ring or strop made from a single strand of rope, with neither end visible (581E). When laying this strand around itself, be sure to see that the two end 'thirds' – 581A yellow (x) and orange (y) – are longer than the central third – 581A black (z) –, because they must be long enough to be finished.

When you lay the strand, twist it slightly about itself so that the crimped parts fall naturally into the slot in the black middle strand. Where the outer strands (x and y) meet (581C), finish them as in photograph 561.

One of the old uses for a grommet was to make a strop for a traditional block (611C).

A cut splice, made in the standing rigging of working and rescue boats in particular, used to be passed over the masthead to rest on a thicker part (the hounds), and a grommet was often placed above the hounds to prevent the eye from sinking deep into the wood.

In an emergency, grommets can be used when gluing or fishing a broken or damaged spar. Make a number of them to fit closely round the spar, and hammer in wooden wedges to make them grip it really tightly.

GROMMET WORKED AS A HANDLE FOR A SHIP'S CHEST 591

1

SOME FUN WITH GROMMETS 601, 602, 611

You make a twin strop for the headsail sheet out of three grommets. Take a piece of rope of suitable thickness, and a good three times as long as the strop required. Use two strands to make two grommets of the same size, and seize (191) each grommet round a large brass or, preferably, lignum vitae thimble, through which the sheet (one end of which is made fast) can run easily. With the third strand, make a grommet which passes through the loops in the other two grommets. With a lanyard, secure the strop to the clew of the headsail, and reeve the sheets through the thimbles.

Make an overhand knot in a strand of manila, work it as a grommet, and you have a small pendant (601C); take an extra turn and you have made a rope grommet (601B) The grommet made up in 601A is to wear as a belt.

Grommets can make rings, napkin rings or bracelets. In these cases, proceed as far as 581D, and then make a decorative knot such as a diamond, star or stopper knot with the four half strands.

Photograph 602 shows a variation of the 'magic knot' on old fishing boats.

1

2

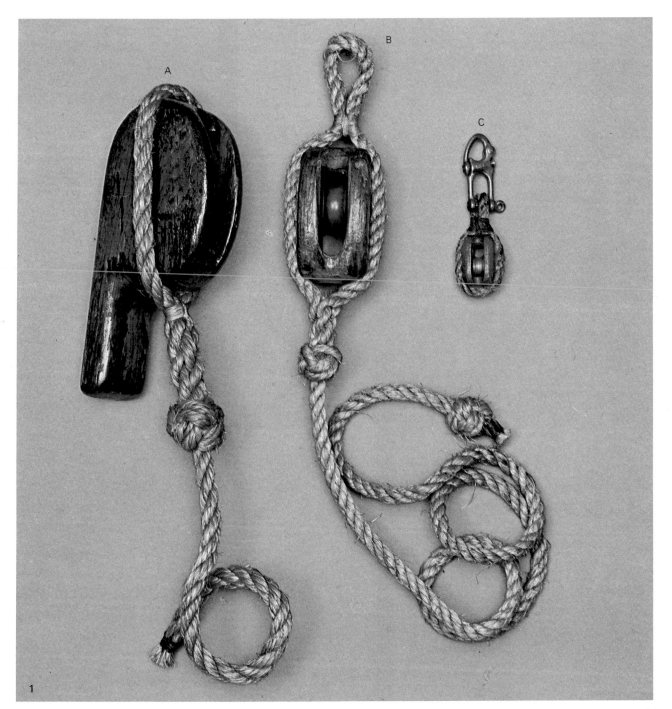

61

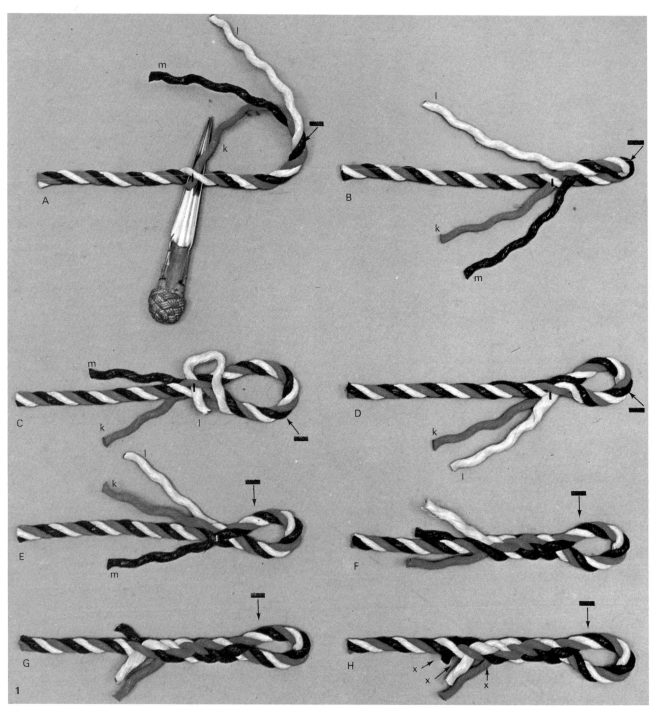

1

EYE SPLICE 621, 631

This splice forms a permanent eye, which could be a large open loop at the end of a mooring line, or a loop tightly spliced round a small thimble. The former must be generous in size, say 20–30 in., if it is required to pass over a commercial bollard.

When learning how to make an eye splice, it is important to master properly the very first tuck that you make with the three working strands (k, l, m, 621A, B, C, D, E). Before starting, mark a circle right round the rope and over all the strands with a felt tip pen (621A, B, C, D, E), know under which strand the tuck should be made. Then do over one, under one, over one, under one, and so on (621F, G, H); pushing the strands through the lay is often hard; three tucks are required in natural fibre rope, and five in synthetic fibre rope. Sellotape will hold the ends of the strands firm when threading them.

A splice looks better, and with synthetic fibre rope is definitely stronger, when tapered (631), (x) in photographs 621H, 631 and 711A, B.

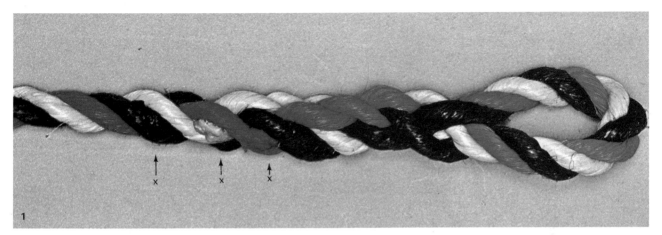

2

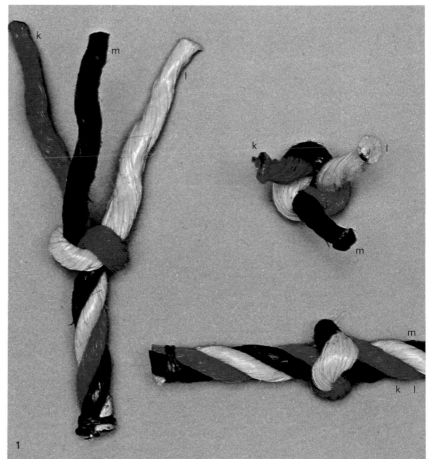

CROWN KNOT 642, 651, 1001

Before making the crown knot, look at photographs 1001A and B. The strands (642 k, l, m and 651 k, l, m) emerge at the sides of the knot.

WALL KNOT 641, 981

Before making the wall knot, look at photographs 981A and B. The strands (641 k, l, m) emerge in the centre of the knot.

BACK SPLICE 651

Start with a crown knot, and then tuck each strand three times. A back splice is made to prevent the end of a rope from unlaying. When made at the end of a rope for a fender, it stops the rope from slipping out of your hand.

1

y
D
E
F
G
x
1

1   H   I   J   K

PINEAPPLE KNOT 661, 671, 681, 691

A decorative way of making the end of a rope thicker is to make a pineapple knot, and it can also be used at the end of a heaving line if you weigh it in the middle.

If you look at the photographs closely, you can see that it is actually a back splice, followed round. You must leave sufficient space initially so that there is room to follow the strands round (x, y, z 661A, B, C and 671D).

First make a back splice (661A, B, C and 671D, E, F, G) by making a crown knot (641 and 651) and tucking the strands twice. Then make a wall knot (681H, I) round the rope, with the three working strands (k, l, m) emerging by the knot, pointing up towards the crown. Follow round half the splice (681J, K) working towards the end, then double the crown knot (691L) at the top and follow the back splice down towards the wall knot (691M, N) which you double (691O). The ends of the strands (691P) can be cut off or worked into the middle of the knot.

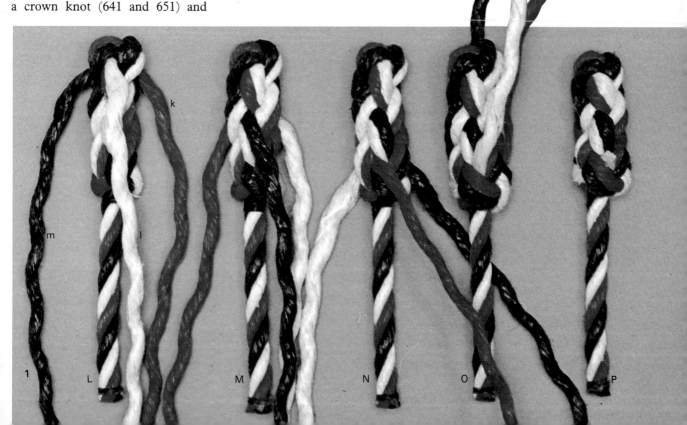

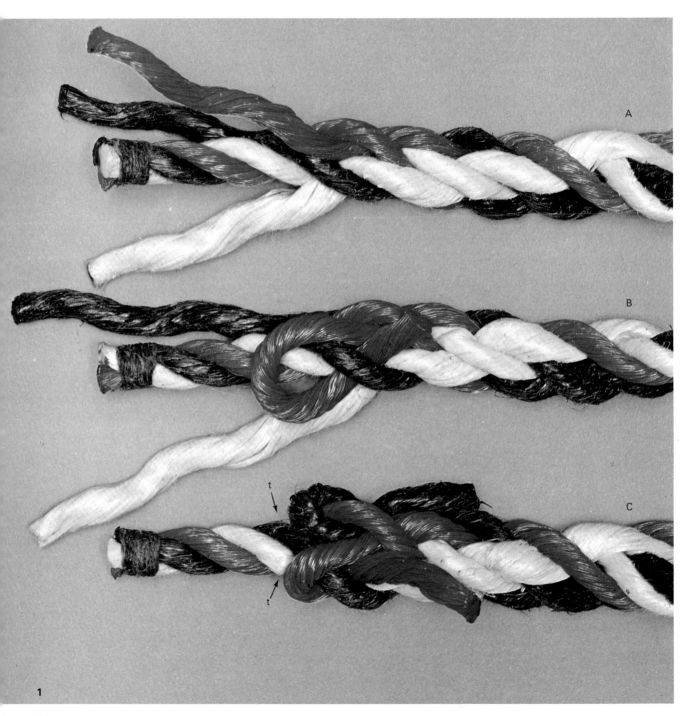

FINISHING SPLICES 711, 701

A splice can be finished in several different ways, depending on its purpose, after the requisite number of tucks has been taken (synthetic fibres five, natural fibres three).

The weakest point of a spliced rope, the point where it will break under load, is just beyond the last tuck where there is the changeover to unspliced rope. It is here that the internal heat caused by friction is concentrated, and this results in the material melting or breaking — arrowed (t).

711A, B At present, the best way of dissipating internal heat is considered to be to taper the splice, and this way of finishing should therefore be preferred. A, with the ends of the strands left sticking out about ¼ in. is the best. If the ends of strands are cut off really close to the rope, as in B, they will jump out when the rope is under load.

711C, D The splice has been finished normally, without tapering. In C about ¼ in. of the strands have been left sticking out, whereas in D the ends have been melted into the space between the strands.

711E Dogging is a traditional method of finishing. Each strand is halved, and the halves of adjacent strands are whipped together (not sewn).

711F The ends of the strands are turned back and tucked once (see 701). They can then be dogged as in 711E.

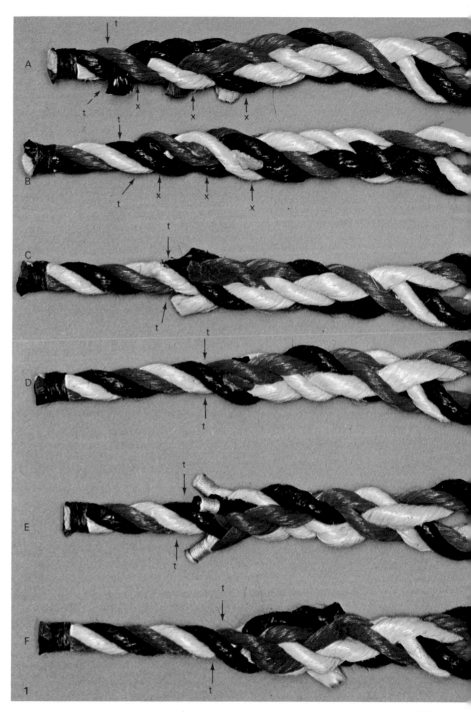

71

1   A   B   C

MANROPE
KNOT   721–731

The manrope knot and the stopper knot look so alike that they can be confused. They are also used for the same purpose, namely to thicken the end of a line permanently so as to ensure that it does not unreeve through an eye, loop or block, or slip out of your hand. The manrope knot, as its name indicates, is used primarily for the manrope, which is a rope handrail led through stanchions along a gangway. The knot may also be used on shore at the end of a rope handrail on a staircase. Instead of a wooden or steel rail on the coachroof, large diameter rope can be rove through the handrail eyes and finished with manrope knots.

Remember the following verse, and you will be sure to make a manrope knot rather than a stopper knot:

First a wall, then a crown

Now tuck up, then stick down

Start with the wall knot (721A), as in photographs 641 and 981; crown it (721B) as in photographs 641, 651 and 1001, and then follow around the wall knot (721C). There are now

72

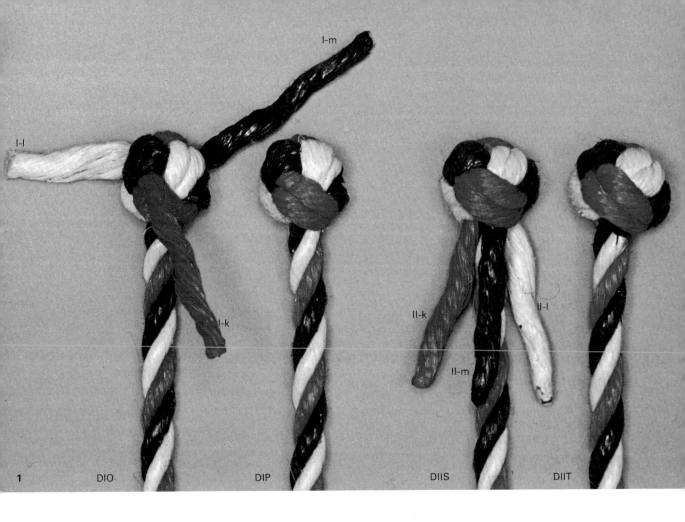

1   DIO.   DIP   DIIS   DIIT

two alternatives; either double the crown and let the strands (Ik, Il, Im) emerge at the sides of the knot (731DIO) or double the crown and tuck the strands (IIk, IIl, IIm) across through the centre of the knot and along the rope (731DIIS). Finish by cutting off the ends close by the knot (731DIP and 731DIIT).

If the knot is to rest continuously against a stanchion or eye, 731DIP is preferable because in 731DIIT the strands could possibly be pushed up and the knot work slightly loose.

When making the manrope knot in the middle of a rope, rather than at the end, do not bring the strands out at the sides (721C) when doubling the wall knot (k, l, m) but tuck them right through the knot so that they emerge on top, centrally above the crown knot (as in 751DIIS). The crown is therefore NOT doubled. Re-lay the strands, and finish with a sewn whipping.

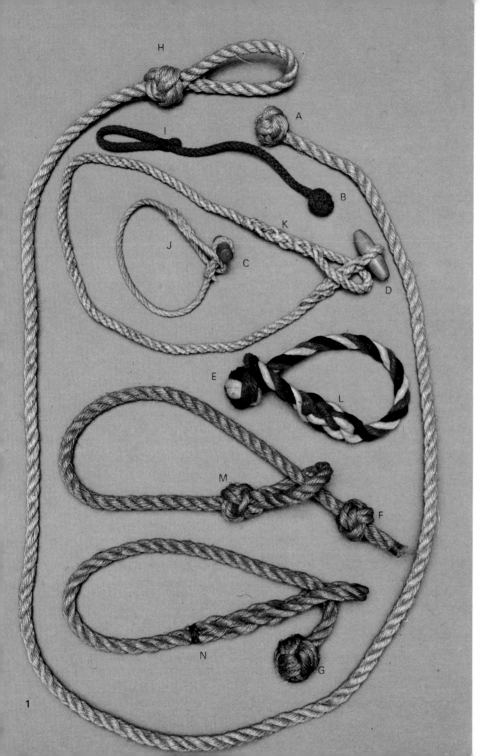

KNOB-AND-EYE and TOGGLE-AND-EYE STROP 741

Photograph 741 shows a variety of strops with spliced toggles (C, D), knob knots (A, E, F, G) and a monkey's fist (B) which is at one end of a line, and which has an eye at the other. In F a diamond knot is made as a stopper knot.

The eye can be made with a stopper knot (741H, M as in photograph 761) or you can use a flat seizing (I), an eye splice (J, K), a whipped eye splice (N) or a back-tucked eye splice (L).

For eye splice see 621: stopper knot 751: monkey's fist 431: diamond knot 781–791: eye splice with stopper knot 761: flat seizing 191: whipping 161 or 181: back-tucked eye splice 701.

STOPPER KNOT 751

A stopper knot may be made as in photograph 751 in a rope that must not slip through a block or out of your hands. Make a crown knot (751A) and follow this with a wall knot beneath it (751B). Follow round the crown knot first (751C), and then the wall knot (751DIO, DIIS). When you follow round the wall knot, the strands (Ik, Il, Im) may either be brought out at the sides and cut off, or through the centre of the knot so that they emerge centrally above the crown (751DIIS). The strands can then either be re-laid (751DIIT) and whipped (161 or 181), or cut off close (751DIIU).

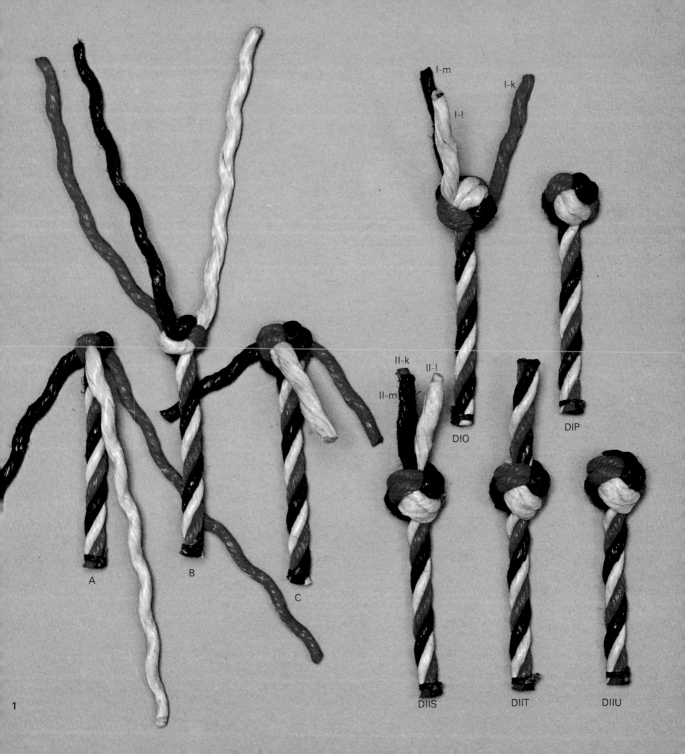

1

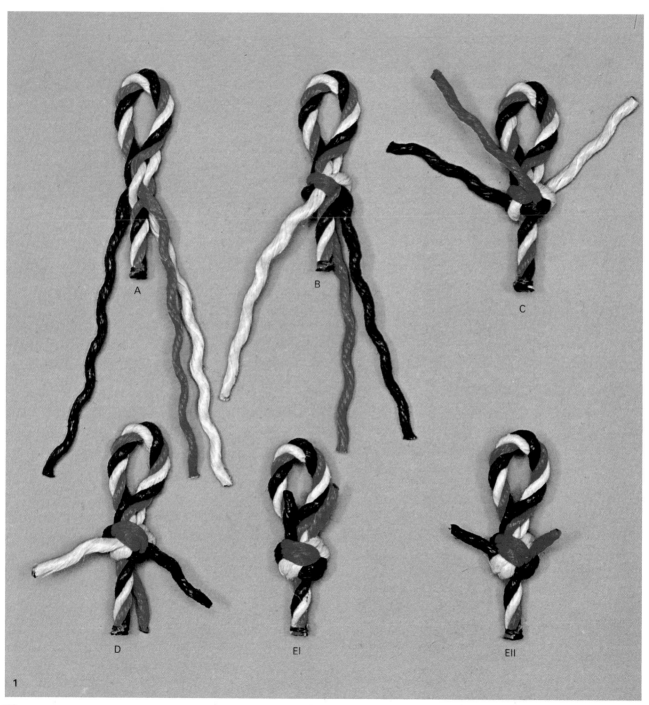

A

B

C

D

EI

EII

1

EYE SPLICE WITH
STOPPER KNOT 761

Tuck the strands as for an eye splice (621A, B, C, D, E, 761A). Then make a wall knot (641, 981) round the rope, and below that a crown knot as in photographs 642, 651 and 1001–761C. Then follow round the wall (761D) and after that the crown. You now have two alternatives; either take the strands through the middle of the knot to emerge close by the first tuck (as in 761EI) or let them emerge at the sides (761EII). Finish by cutting off the ends. The knot is in fact the same as that in 721–731.

As you can see in photographs 741H and M, this knot can also be used for a knob-and-eye strop. If you pass the end through a small eye or something similar before completing both ends of a strop of this sort, it will prevent the eye splice from becoming jammed in a block, or being pulled right through a larger aperture.

A knob-and-eye strop can be passed through a hole bored in the base of a cleat, so that you can hang a halyard up with it to keep the deck and cockpit clear of rope.

In photograph 772 a tackle (b) with an eye in the end is rove through a block (c) to which the halyard (d) is secured; the stopper knot (a) beneath the eye splice prevents the eye from being pulled through the block when the sail is hoisted. When the eye is hooked over a cleat, hauling on the tail of the runner almost doubles the power applied to the halyard.

The rope on the left, 771, has been decorated by making an ornamental stopper knot after making an eye splice. The wall knot alone was followed round before the strands were cut off short.

1

2

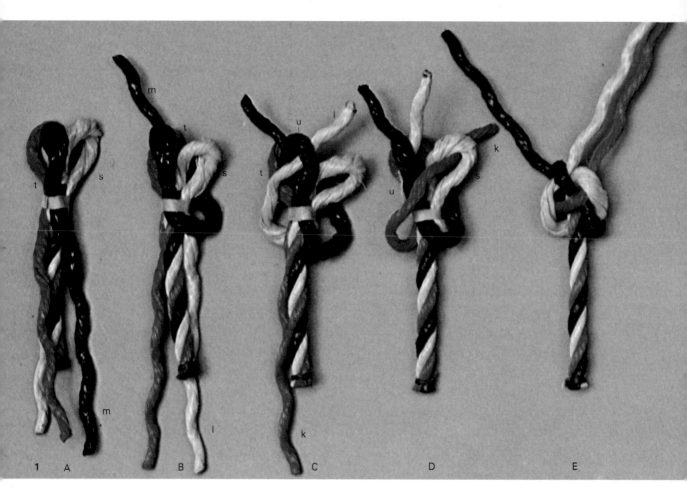

1   A   B   C   D   E

DIAMOND
KNOT 781–791

The diamond knot, made of three (single rope) or six (doubled rope) strands, is a firm, strong stopper knot, and has many applications as an ornamental knot.

If you put doubled diamond knots 12 in. apart in a long thick rope, you make a climbing rope. Take two similar ropes and link them with wooden treads that rest on diamond knots, and you have a rope ladder.

You can also make a hanging book case with a horizontal plank. If you make the knot with six strands in large diameter doubled manila and fluff out the strands where they emerge beneath the knot, you can hang it near the washbasin and keep combs, tiepins and hairpins in the tassel (1151A). Make it in this doubled rope, and you will have little pendants or dusting brushes (1181C, D and 1191A).

Lash or tape the three strands to the rope so that the bights are kept open (781A). Pass strand (m) round the adjacent bight (s) and lead it up through the next bight (t) (781B). Then pass the next strand (l) outside the adjacent bight (t), and lead it up through the next bight (u) (781C). The third strand (k) is taken round and outside its neighbour (u), and up through bight (s) (781D). Haul the knot tight careful-

1   F   G   H   I   J

ly (781D, E) until you have made a single diamond knot (791H) with the strands emerging from the centre of the knot (791I). The strands can either be cut off, or re-laid and finished with a sewn whipping (181, 791J).

An alternative way of making a diamond knot is to start with a crown knot (651C). Pull the orange strand (k) out of the black bight, take it round outside the black bight, and then pass it beneath the yellow bight so that it lies next to the black strand (m). Pull the black strand (m) out of the yellow bight, take it outside the yellow bight and beneath the orange bight to lie next to the yellow strand (l). Pull the yellow strand (l) out of the orange bight, and lead it under the black bight. You are now at stage 781E, ready to haul the strands tight to make the single diamond knot (791F). Follow the strands round and finish as described above.

MATTHEW WALKER   811

The Matthew Walker, though simple to make, is very difficult to pull tight. Traditionally it is often used for a line attached to a bucket, a single Matthew Walker being made on the freshwater bucket line, and a double Matthew Walker on the saltwater bucket line so as to prevent confusion at night.

The Matthew Walker can also be made as a stopper knot in a lanyard.

Among other things, lanyards were rove between deadeyes so as to tauten stays and shrouds, and the knot was then usually made in four-stranded hemp.

The Matthew Walker can also be used when making a comb-holder (1151B), a crumb or dusting brush (1191A) and, in thin line, a small pendant.

1

2

A1 A2 B1 B2

1 A B

STAR KNOT 821–831

Many books describe the star knot as difficult, but if you have a good look at the entire sequence first, and do not hurry over each successive stage, it will not be long before you have this star among knots at your finger tips. Rush at it, and you will be frustrated and find it difficult.

The star knot can be used in the making of many things, comb-holders, pendants, stoppers, earrings, door knobs, drawer-pulls etc.

The knot can be made with any number of strands, and the more there are the thicker and more decorative will the knot be.

Start anticlockwise with a variation of the wall knot (822A1, A2) and crown this backwards (821B1, B2) working clockwise as in photograph 1001B. Then follow around the 'wall knot' (831C, C1, C2) bringing the strands (Ck, Cl, Cm) out centrally on top of the knot. Now follow around the crown knot (831D, D1, E, F, F1); the strands (Ek, El, Em) emerge below the knot

82

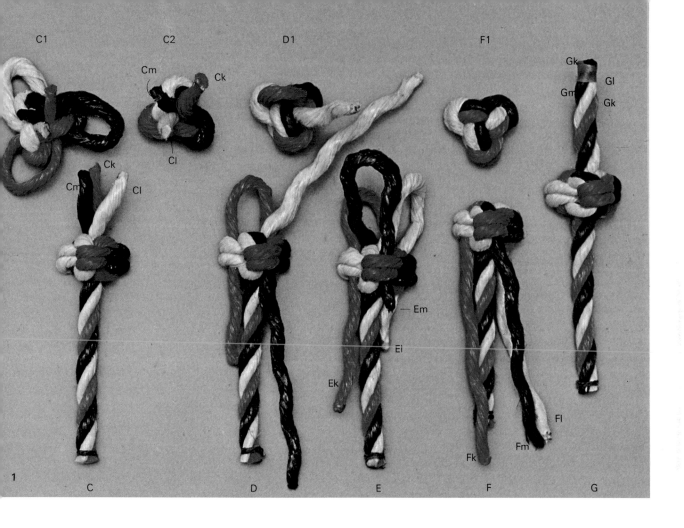

C1　　　　C2　　　　D1　　　　F1

Cm　　Ck

Cl

Ck

Cm　　Cl

Gk
Gl
Gm
Gk

Em

Ei

Ek

Fl

Fm

Fk

1

C　　　　D　　　　E　　　　F　　　　G

(831E), and are pulled tight (Fk, Fl, Fm), lying parallel and close to the rope (831F). The next step is to follow the adjacent bight, and tuck the working strands (Gk, Gl, Gm) up into the heart of the knot. You then re-lay the strands and apply a sewn (181) or common (161) whipping (831G).

Instead of re-laying the strands as in 831G, you can crown the knot normally, anticlockwise (1001a) and tuck the strands down again to emerge parallel to the rope underneath the knot where you cut off the ends.

If you make these six strands into a loop, you have a button which can be passed through a becket to close an object such as a coat, cardigan, satchel, or sack, or can be used to close an opening in an awning or tent; you sew the button and loop on to one side of the opening and the becket to match it on the other half. A further alternative for this purpose is a knob-and-eye strop.

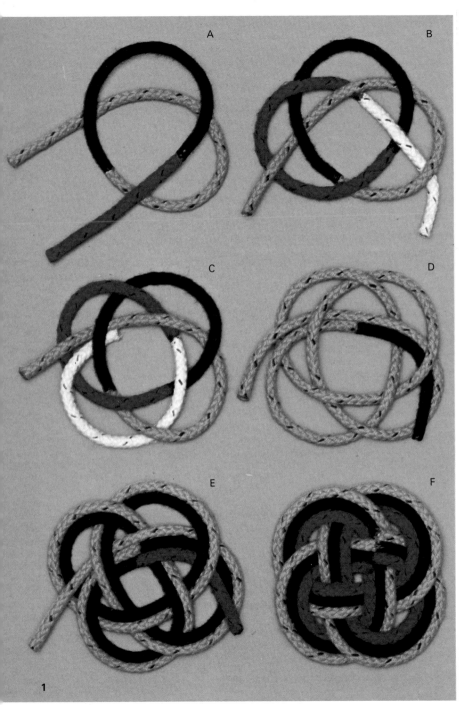

CARRICK MAT 841

When making mats, you can use up cordage that has deteriorated and is no longer strong enough for its original purpose, but is too good to throw away. The usable pieces are cut out of the line or rope, and are knotted together for mat-making, with the result that no expensive rope goes to waste.

CARRICK MAT   851

A mat can be placed on deck round an eye bolt to prevent the block from damaging the deck, and to reduce the noise when it falls (852). Smaller mats can be placed beneath glasses (842) and mugs, while larger ones can be put on the dining table beneath pans and dishes.

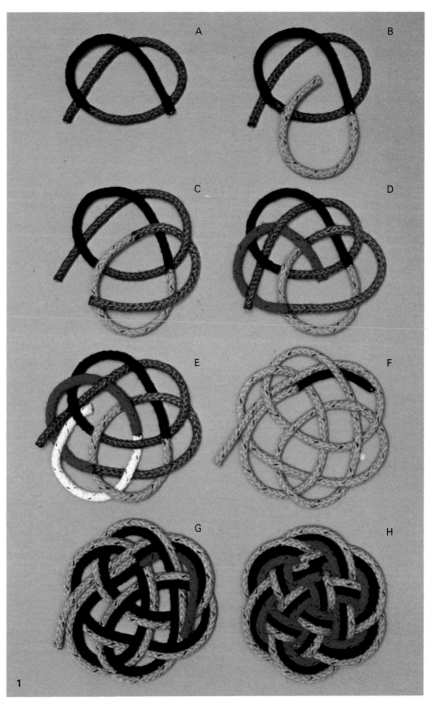

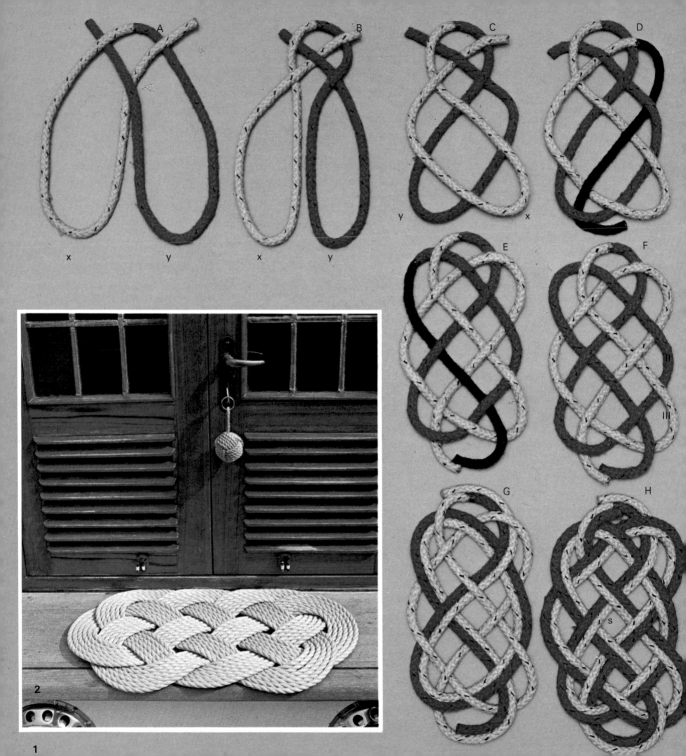

A

B

C

D

E

F

G

H

x   y   x   y   y   x   II   III   s

1

2

OCEAN MAT 861

Clifford W. Ashley calls this an Ocean Plat in his bible *The Ashley Book of Knots*, whereas in their *Encyclopedia of Knots and Fancy Rope Work* Van Raoul Graumont and John Hensel call it 'The Sailor's True Lover Mat Weave', and Charles L. Spencer in *Knots, Splices and Fancy Work* includes it under Ocean Plaits or Mats as 'Oval Mat'. It is therefore a mat with several names and a variety of uses; furthermore it can be made with different lengths.

The simplest Ocean or Oval Mat is shown in photograph 861. The series of photographs needs no explanation, but it does help if you start by making full-scale enlarged drawings on paper of 861A, B, C, D, E, F, with a length to breadth ratio of about 55 : 35. They act as a guide when you are making the mat.

All you have to do is to follow the pattern (861G, H) and finish off, which means sewing the doubled ropes to each other with needle and thread.

The mat on the bridgedeck shown in photograph 862 is made of ⅜ in. manila-colored polypropylene. After plaiting, tightening, following round five times and working out excess loops, I had about 16 ft. left of the original 80 ft. of rope. You can make a mat about 21 × 12 in. in size with about 65 ft. of rope.

Instead of sewing the doubled ropes together, I smeared the bottom with a layer of silicone glue. Although this makes the mat rather smooth underneath, this is effective in practice if the mat is laid between raised edges, say on a gangplank or on a teak deck.

The key-ring tag in photograph 862 is a monkey's fist with a cork core, followed round five times.

A Turk's Head-type ocean mat can be made by putting a spar or large rope through the quadrilateral centre point marked S (861H). When the bights are hauled good and tight round this core, the result is a decorative armband with two plaited rosettes.

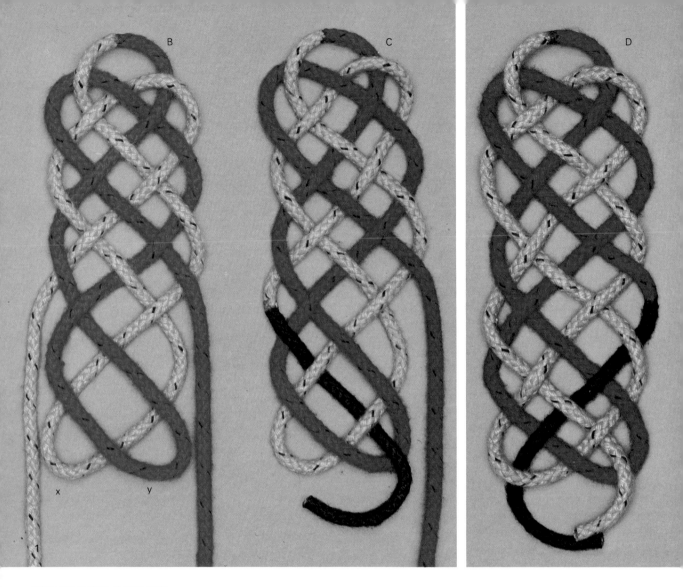

SIX BIGHT OCEAN
MAT   871–881–891

The length of the ocean mat can be increased as required, say to make a sort of runner for the sole or for a gangway. Note that this mat is three bights longer (891E, I, II, III, IV, V, VI) than the mat in 861F (I, II, III), while the mat in 892 is six

bights long already but will be extended to nine.

Be sure to see that the two loops (x and y) in photograph 861A, B, C are so long that, when the ocean mat has been made up to and including stage 861E, F, further bights can

still be formed (871A x, y and 881 x, y) so as to lengthen the mat. The last stage of the ordinary mat, 861F, matches the start at 871A. The mat is completed in the same way as the ordinary ocean mat (881B, C, D, E – 861C, D, E, F).

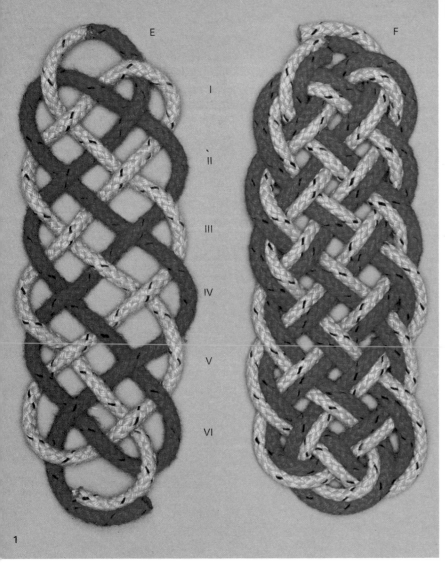

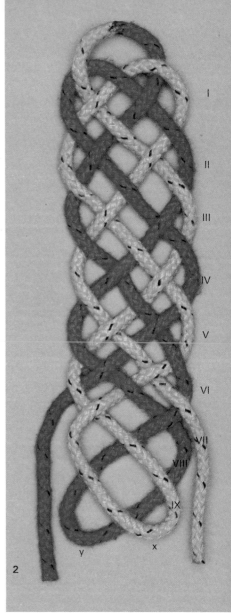

NINE BIGHT OCEAN MAT 892

When making the nine-bight ocean mat, be sure to see that loops (x) and (y) in 861A, B, C are even longer than is needed for the six-bight ocean mat. 892, with working loops (x) and (y), matches the final stage of 881D–891E. Finishing poses no extra problems.

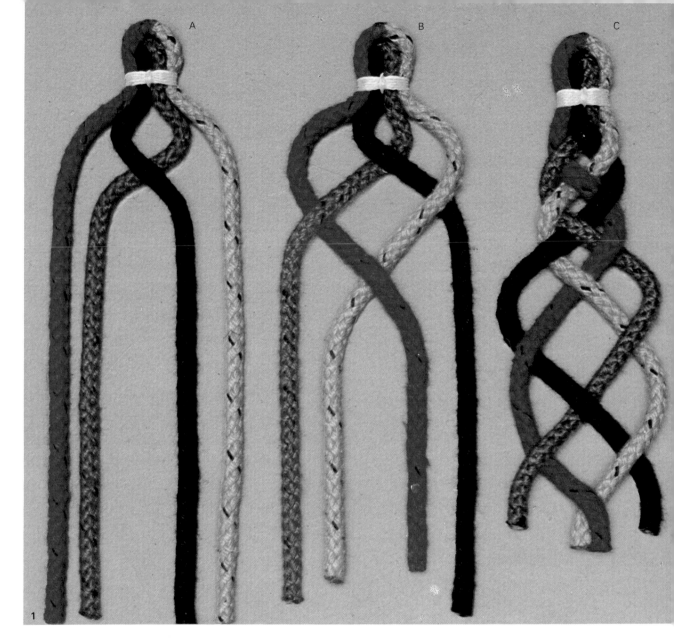

1

FOUR STRAND FRENCH SENNIT 901–911

Plaited bands or cords can be used for decorative purposes when a result required is a belt or strap.

SIX STRAND FRENCH SENNIT 912

Unlay the strands of $\frac{1}{2}$ in. diameter line for a length of 5 ft., and whip the line carefully to ensure that it

does not unlay any further. Halve the three strands to make six small strands, and plait these (912). When the sennit is long enough, make pairs of half strands into three

strands, and whip the three-stranded line just beyond the end of the sennit. You can now splice the sennit to make a large loop (621). The ends of the splice are secured to the line/splice with a sewn whipping (181).

If you make a running Turk's Head (1061 or 1071), you can pull the loop tight round something and make the end of the rope fast to another object for instance when hauling a heavy object up the side of a vessel (or a building or slope).

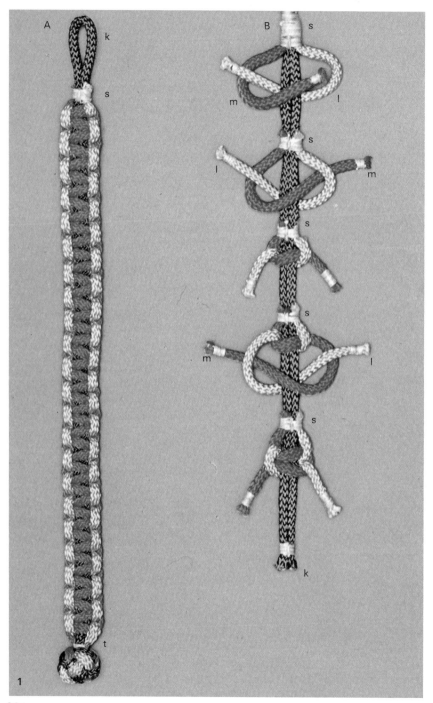

PORTUGUESE FLAT SENNIT 921

You could ask at this point whether this is seaman's work or just handicrafts — but in fact it is both. Macramé, as this type of ropework is called, is used to maintain a ship.

To start the Portuguese flat sennit (921), double the core (k), leaving a loop that is large enough to take the button at the other end, and make a flat seizing (s) (191) round the core and the cords that you will be knotting. Make overhand knots round the core, as shown in 921B, until the sennit is as long as you require, when you finish it with a second flat seizing.

There are 44 knots on the bracelet in 922A, and it is finished with a manrope knot (721–731).

Material required: $\frac{1}{16}$ in. cotton cord, as is used for anorak drawstrings; green 2 ft., yellow and orange $3\frac{1}{2}$ in. each. This will make a bracelet about $8\frac{1}{2}$ in. in length between button and loop.

FLAT HITCH SENNIT 931

This consists of a core, around which half hitches are made with two cords alternately. First double the core (k), and make a flat seizing round the loop and the two knotting cords (l, m) at (s). Make the loop big enough to take the button at the other end. The half hitches round the core are made clockwise with the red cord and anticlockwise with the orange cord (931B). After making 55 half hitches, seize the core and knotting cords again at (t). Now make a Matthew Walker (811), cut the ends off level, and put on a common (161) or sewn (181) whipping.

Material: $\frac{1}{16}$ in. cotton cord, 28 in. green and 36 in. each of red and orange, will make a band about 8 in. long between loop and knot.

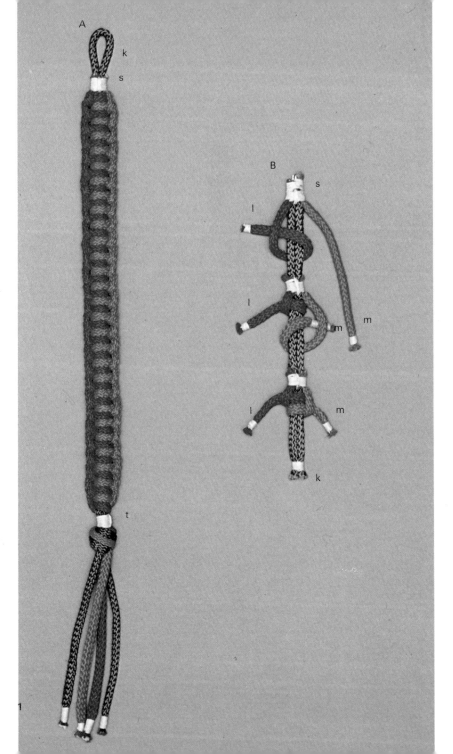

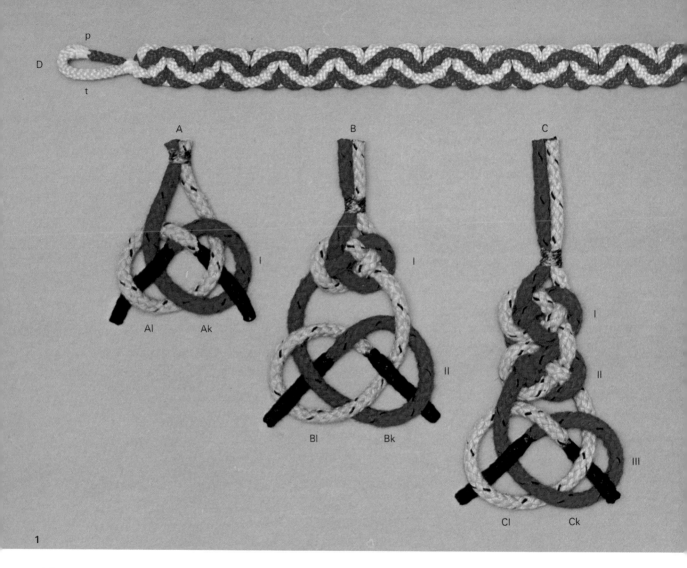

DOUBLE CARRICK BEND
SENNIT 941

This is suitable for making a belt or strap. Sew two cords of different colours together (p) and seize them (191) leaving a loop big enough to take the knob at the other end of the belt (941D). Then knot the strap by making a series of alternate carrick

bends (351), the first bight being made with the red cord (Ak) above the yellow (Al–941A), while succeeding and alternate bends are made with the yellow cord (Bl) above the red (Bk). The result is 941BII and 941CII (tight). When each hitch has been made it is

hauled tight. Continue with red (Ck) over yellow (Cl–941CIII) and so on, repeating this until the strap length is right. Then seize the two ends together as in 351 (arrow on 951D) and cover the seizing with a stevedore knot (page 95).

CHAIN PLAIT 951

After finishing the carrick bends, you can use up the remaining metre of red cord by chain plaiting. First make a stevedore's knot (at the arrow) to cover the seizing; to do this at stage 211A make a full round turn round the standing part before continuing as in 211B, C, D. Seven-

teen chain hitches provide a strap about 8 in. long, which is finished as in 951F (front) and G (back view). The rest of the cord will make a two-part monkey's fist (431). The belt is now about 2½ ft. long, and is done up by pushing the monkey's fist through the loop, or by making

a sheet bend (32II) with the chain plait, with the knot beneath.

To make the belt you require 8 ft. yellow and 13 ft. red braided polypropylene, ⅛ in. in diameter, and some thin wire for the seizings.

ROUND SENNIT 961, 971

The round sennit is interesting when you want something which is a change from a normal rope, but not too intricate. Among other things it can be used to make a handrail for steps, or as curtain cord, bell cord, electric light switch pull cord and so on. This, the easiest of round sennits, is suitable for a lanyard, for a whistle or knife, or a safety line for tools, marline spike or fid when made with thin twine. If you look closely at the photographs, you will see that photograph 961 shows a proper plait, but 971 does not.

Turn A: yellow to the right, *above* black to the left
Turn B: green upwards, *left* of red downwards
Turn C: yellow to the left *above* black to the right
Turn D: green downwards *left* of red upwards
5th turn as A: yellow to the right *above* black to the left
6th turn as B, 7th as C and so on.

You can start the sennit with a loop and finish it with a decorative knot, with or without a tassel made by combing out the ends.

The photograph in 971 is of a two-stranded laid rope with each strand made up of two lines. Red and yellow are twisted right-handed (Z twist) about each other, and black and green are twisted similarly. These two right-handed bicolour strands are laid left-handed about each other to form an S-twist rope.

Turn A: yellow to the right *above* black to the left
Turn B: green upwards *left* of red downwards

Turn C: yellow to the left *below* black to the right

Turn D: green downwards to the *right* of red upwards

5th as A: 6th as B: 7th as C and so on.

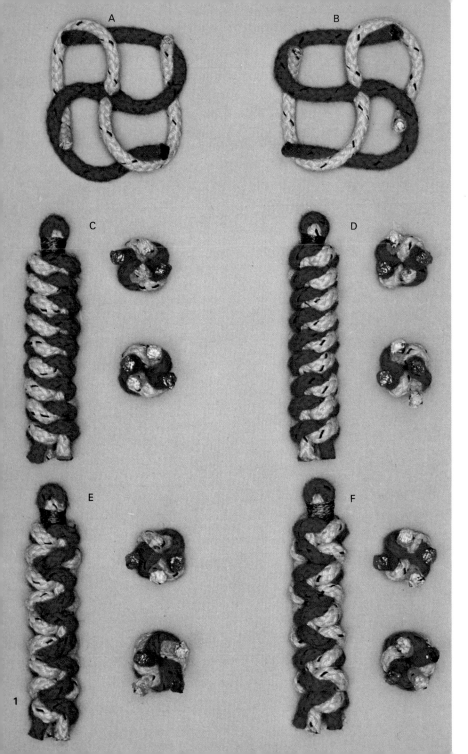

WALL PLAIT 981

Wall plaiting is often used when making the bell toggle, a key pendant, or a pull cord for the snap on the spinnaker boom end fitting. It is also very useful when you are trying to open or close a zip fastener with clammy fingers in cold wet weather. The wall plait can be made anti-clockwise (981A) or clockwise (981B); combinations of the two are also possible. The end can be finished with a flat seizing (191), by making a decorative knot in the end, or by tucking the ends away inside. The following alternatives are shown in 981:

	1st	2nd	3rd	4th	5th	
C	l	l	l	l	l	and so on
D	r	r	r	r	r	and so on
E	l	r	l	r	l	and so on
F	r	l	r	l	r	and so on

l = anticlockwise (981A): r = clockwise (981B)

WALL AND CROWN
PLAIT 991, 992

The wall plait (981) and the crown
plait (1001) can also be combined to
form a wall and crown plait, which
can be used for the same purposes
as the other two plaits. Only the
pattern and the appearance differ.

	1st	2nd	3rd
991 1	WCL	CCL	WCL
991 2	WCL	CCR	WCL

4th	5th	
CCL	WCL	and so on
CCR	WCL	and so on

W = wall: C = crown:
L = anticlockwise: R = clockwise

The pattern can be changed as you
wish.

1

2

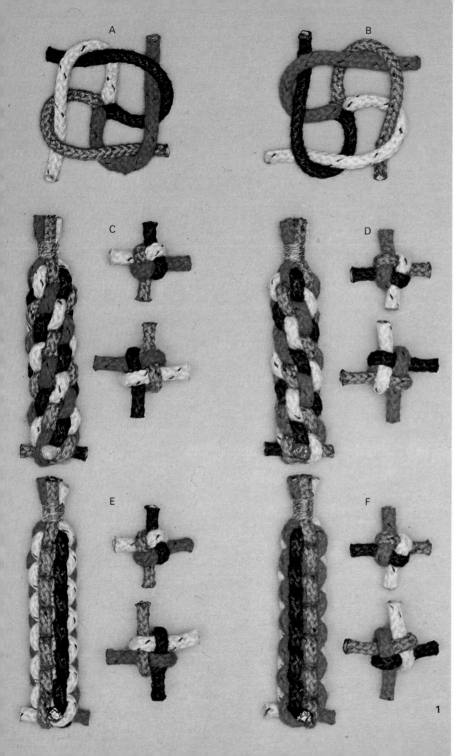

CROWN PLAIT 1001

The crown knot plait is often used to make fenders and bell toggles, and it is also suitable for all the applications listed under wall plait. It can be made anticlockwise (1001A) or clockwise (1001B), or a combination of the two.

	1st	2nd	3rd	4th	5th	
C	l	l	l	l	l	and so on
D	r	r	r	r	r	and so on
E	l	r	l	r	l	and so on
F	r	l	r	l	r	and so on

l = anticlockwise 1001A: r = clockwise 1001B

The ends can be finished with a simple wall knot, followed by a decorative knot, or by seizing the lines below the wall knot and combing out the strands into a tassel, or by tucking the ends into the plait and cutting them off after the wall knot has been made.

WALL AND CROWN KNOTTING 1011, 1021

1011A: double the rope

1st turn: anticlockwise wall knot

12 turns: clockwise crown knots

14th turn: anticlockwise wall knot

15th turn: clockwise crown knot

16th turn: follow around the wall knot

17th turn: follow around the crown knot

Cut off the ends above the crown knot, close to the plait.

1

1

1011B: double the rope
    1st turn: anticlockwise wall knot
    2nd turn: clockwise wall knot
    3rd turn: anticlockwise crown knot
    Repeat 2nd and 3rd turns five times more
    14th turn: anticlockwise wall knot
    15th turn: clockwise crown knot
    16th turn: follow around the wall knot
    17th turn: follow around the crown knot

Cut the ends above the crown knot, close to the plait.

1021C: double the rope
    11 turns: anticlockwise wall knots
    12th turn: clockwise crown knot
    13th turn: follow round the wall knot
    14th turn: follow round the crown knot

Cut off the ends.

1021D: double the rope
    1st turn: anticlockwise wall knot
    2nd turn: clockwise wall knot
    Repeat 1st and 2nd turns four more times
    11th turn: anticlockwise wall knot
    12th turn: clockwise crown knot
    13th turn: follow around the wall knot and cut ends

The rope was too short to double the crown knot. When making decorative knots with scraps of rope, you always have to improvise.

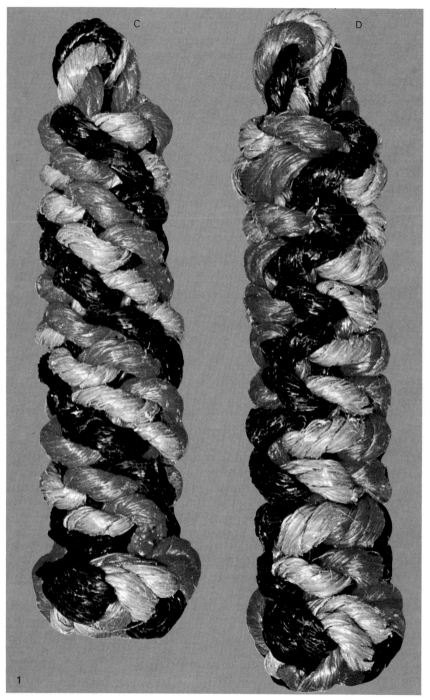

C

D

USING SCRAP ROPE 1031

A: Seize (191) two doubled manila ropes. Unlay the twelve strands and re-lay the middle strands of all four ropes to form an internal core. With the other eight strands, make a wall plait anticlockwise around the core. If you have enough rope, make another wall knot with four alternate strands. Beneath this whip (161) all the eight strands that you have been walling, and cut them off. With the four remaining strands that form the core, make a crown plait (1001A, B, E) with the last crown knot made anticlockwise. You follow with stage 831C only of the star knot. Whip (161) the strands which emerge centrally, and fluff out the tail into a tassel.

B: I found a piece of tarred manila among marina rubbish, and from this I made a short fender for the dinghy. Double the rope and make a crown plait with the six strands (1001A, B, E). Finish with a clockwise wall knot (981B) and firmly seize (191) the strands which emerge centrally.

C: This plait is made of tight clockwise and anticlockwise crown knots (1001A, B, E), finished with two whippings.

D: The wall plait (981A, C) tends to stretch somewhat lengthwise, and is therefore not so suitable for plaiting fenders.

1

A   B   C   D

1

103

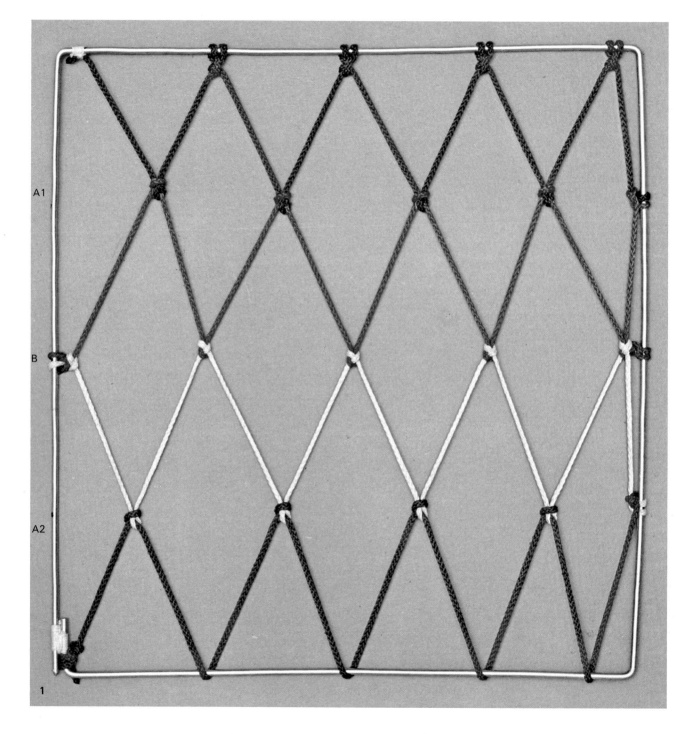

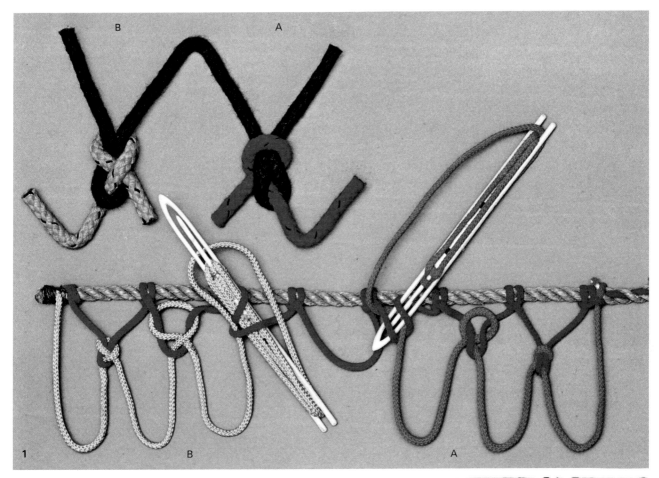

NETTING 1041, 1051

Netting is used on board to fill the space between the guardrail and the deck, and for stowage purposes, such as above a berth. A round net can be used as a light sailbag, and shopping bags can also be made out of round nets.

For the guardrail net, a clove hitch is made round the lifeline above each square of mesh. The bottom of the net is led through a hole in the toerail.

Flat nets, such as 1041 and 1051, are made with the sheet bend (321), and this may be made in two ways; when working from left to right the sheet bend is made in front of the loop (1041B, 1051B), but when you work from right to left it is made behind the loop (1041A and 1051A).

1

TURK'S HEAD 1061

When making a Turk's Head, hold the rope firmly at the crossing points marked O. When the first set has been completed (108A1), follow around again once to make a two-part (108AII) or twice for a three-part (1081AIII) Turk's head. The knot is generally three-part.

TURK'S HEAD WITH AN EXTRA TURN 1071

Again hold the rope with your thumb at the places marked O. When you are making the Turk's Head, you will realize which are the crossing points to hold. Turk's Heads are often made round a guardrail or some other object: see photograph 1081C.

After completing the first set (H), you can follow around again once (1081BII), twice (108BIII) or three (1081BIV) or more times.

1   A   B   C

USES FOR THE TURK'S HEAD 1081 and 1091

- To decorate glasses (1091).
- Stoppers on a horse (1092). This is only half a Turk's Head, the knot only being made up to and including stage 1071 D, E. Haul it really tight, and follow the turns around once or twice.
- Hand grip on the tiller.
- Marker on the king spoke of the steering wheel. This points upwards when the rudder is amidships.
- Stopper round the forestay above the bottom splice or terminal; prevents the lowest jib hank from dropping down and jamming.
- Hand grip on the stile of a mop, or on a boathook or quant.
- Necktie ring (1232) or napkin ring.
- Decoration round a post, stanchion, thick rope, ladder etc.
- Grip round a knife handle or a hammer.
- To ornament or mark your tools.
- As a running Turk's Head, so that the size of a loop can be altered.
- Flattened out, as a small mat.
- To start or finish a whipping.
- To make a little cap at the thick end of the marline spike or fid.
- Round an oar as a stopper by the rowlock.
- As a transition between two plaits on a bell toggle.

2

1

ROPE LADDER 1101

This photograph shows a way of making a ladder to use when you swim from the boat. Take some strong rope, about $\frac{1}{2}$ in. in diameter, double it and make a firm flat seizing (191). Continue as in photograph 1101, until you have as many rungs as you require. Be sure to see that the rungs are wide enough to take boots; depending on the thickness of the rope you will need to make 10–15 round turns in order to obtain a width of about 5–6 in. The rungs should be about 1 ft. apart.

You can strengthen the rungs by inserting a piece of broomstick or pipe, and the bottom rung should always be weighted to prevent it from floating. In practice it is best if two rungs at least are underwater, with the third just above the surface.

The same knot can be used with thin cord to make a special belt, bracelet or watch-strap, with an eye at one end and a decorative knot at the other. In order to make the knot, make a flat seizing (191) at the appropriate place, adding a third piece of cord at this point so that you have three lines with which to make a small button.

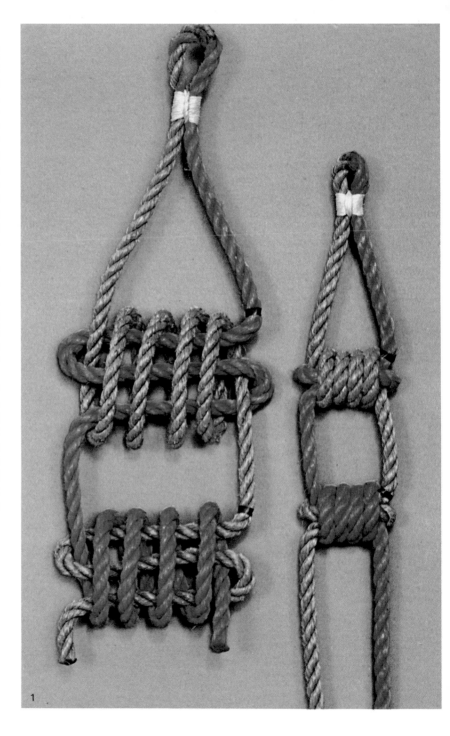

1

HALF HITCHING A FENDER 1111

Instead of making a fender out of crown knots (1001) you can cover one with a rope mesh; the fender could be an old one with its bottom rotted as a result of being trailed in the water, or a plastic one that you want to camouflage.

You start by making a round turn in the rope; on this make back-to-front half hitches (as in 233) so that you have a ring on which are the necessary number of half hitches. Continue spirally, making each new half hitch through a previous hitch. To increase the size, you can make two hitches through one hitch in the previous row.

To decrease: you occasionally skip one hitch of the previous row. This in fact leaves a small hole.

When a new piece of rope is needed, grip the end of it beneath previous rows of half hitches. Hitching succeeding rows over the end of a rope already used up will hold it firm. A good way to finish is to push the end under the cover, which will hold it fast.

1

A

1

2

SERVING and
WHIPPING 1121, 1122, 1131 and 1132

A service is applied to rope, wire rope or other objects in order to protect them from the weather. A steering wheel is whipped, not only for decorative purposes, but to improve the helmsman's grip. A cold metal steering wheel can be whipped in various ways, either by passing the rope round and round the wheel as in 1122, or more decoratively, say with a French spiral whipping as in 1132, or with the three-strand running cockscomb (1121, 1131). You could start by making the line fast with a whipping, and covering it with a Turk's Head (1061, 1071).

The methods used for 1121–1131 and 1132 are actually the same, only

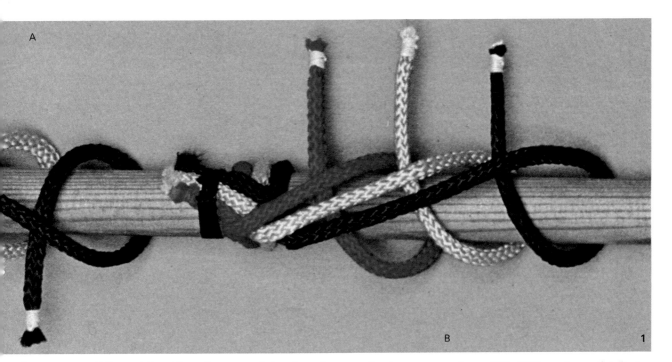

the pattern differs. The French spiral whipping, 1132, is the simplest and consists of a series of half hitches made round the object, so providing a whipping with a spiral rib that runs clockwise round the object. You can of course also make the rib run anticlockwise. Cord was used in the photograph, but any material will serve.

In the three-strand running cockscomb the difference is that the half hitches are made alternately anticlockwise and clockwise in threes (1131B). Ensure that the completed part, with the manrope knot (721–731) on the end, is facing you. The principle of this method is the same, regardless of the number of cords that you use.

BELL TOGGLE or BELL ROPE 1141, 1142

A special bell toggle was hung on the clapper of the bell near the sand glass through which the grains of sand ran from one part to the other in the space of half an hour; during a watch an extra stroke was made on the bell every time that the glass had emptied. For example, the watch starting at 12 noon: glass empty at 12.30 – one stroke on the bell; empty again at 1 o'clock – two strokes; empty for the third time – three strokes at 1.30, and so on. At four o'clock, eight bells, the new watch came up on deck. In the course of time the bell toggle became a show piece for seamanship on ships. Today a bell toggle is more often seen in bars, the bell being rung for last rounds to be ordered just before closing time!

COMB HOLDER 1151

This is merely a decorative knot made in large-diameter manila or sisal rope, with the strands untwisted below the knot. The tail is trimmed into shape, and may be hung near a mirror or washstand. Combs, hairpins, tiepins, brooches etc can be kept in it.

Here a six-strand Matthew Walker has been made.

KNOTS ORNAMENTING A DECANTER 1161

This decanter has been decorated with several of the knots and hitches described in this book; the intention was not to produce something particularly showy, but to combine simple knots in a way that is visually pleasing. Bottles can also be decorated in this way.

KNOTS AND WOOD 1171

Knots are very different when made in wood. Instead of being tied, they are formed with chisel, gouge, knife, file and sandpaper. Throughout the ages, knots have often been used decoratively (1121). Those on the opposite page were carved out of scrap wood, and are mounted in round brass thimbles. The 'knots' actually stand under $3\frac{1}{2}$ in. high (half the size here).

1

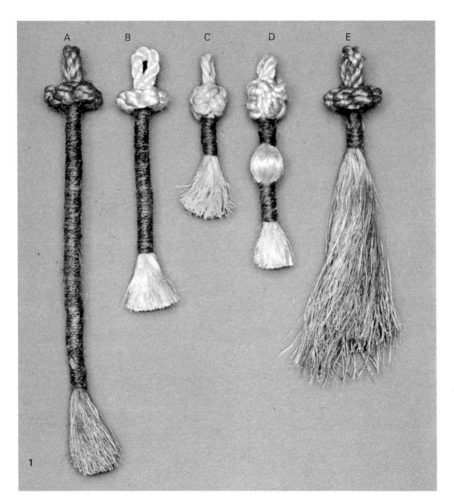

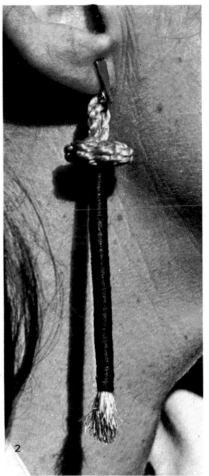

SMALL PENDANTS –
EAR-RINGS – DUSTING
BRUSH   1181, 1182, 1191

If you have the ability to make two decorative knots, you can produce all these ornaments from scrap pieces of rope!

They have many uses. The very small ones (1181A, B, C, D, E and 1182) can be used as small pendants or ear-rings; the rather larger ones (119A and B) are for use as dusting brushes, key pendants, decorative knots for pulling the lavatory chain or the curtain drawcord, and so on. The rather smaller one (119C) also makes a good pendant.

There is no great expenditure over material. A quarter of an hour's work or so, and you will have made someone happy with a really personal present.

1182: A, B and C, star knots: C and D, diamond knots: E, star knot.
1182: as 1181A, star knot
1191: A, diamond knot: B and C, star knot.

N

NW

NO

W

O

ZW

ZO

Z

1

KEY PENDANTS 1201, 1211

Any ordinary knot, or any decorative knot, can be transformed into a key ring pendant, and you can really let your imagination run riot because the possibilities are boundless. Almost all the tags in this wind rose have monkey's fists (1201 SW, W, NW, N, NE, E, SE). The SW splice is finished as a manrope knot (721–731) and S is a two-rope diamond knot (381–391), the two ends of which are finished with a four-strand manrope knot (721–731); the remaining two strands form the tassel.

KNOTS IN METAL 1221, 1222

Metal is particularly suitable for making knots as ornaments (1221C and 1222A are made of brass rod), as little pendants (1221A is made of a stainless steel split pin), as a special bell toggle (1222B is brass) or as a ring, such as are made by the silversmith and goldsmith Menno Meijer of Gouda.

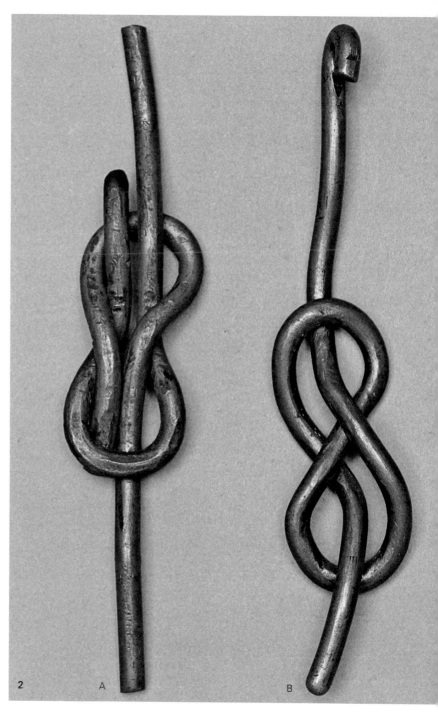

TELEVISION CABLE
KNOT 1231

Many pieces of cable were left in the streets when closed-circuit television came to Amsterdam, and they proved particularly suitable for experimentation. One of the results is this 'transmitting tower-like' knot.

SCARF RING 1232

Many scouts have made a Turk's Head with a leather bootlace, to use as a scarf ring.

2

1

PAPERWEIGHT and
SHOPPING BAG 1241,
1251

Just one of the dozens of other possible ways of making knots, bends, hitches, splices and fancy knots; this is the spritsail sheet bend

(1241).

Also, a smaller reminder of the vast field of macramé, plaiting, net-making, weaving and crochet. The

latter is also a form of knotting, as can be seen from this shopping bag which was crocheted from two-strand twine.

INDEX